European Computer Driving Licence®

ECDL Advanced

Syllabus 2.0

Module AM6 - Presentation

Using Microsoft® PowerPoint 2003

Release ECDL233v1

Published by:

CiA Training Ltd
Business & Innovation Centre
Sunderland Enterprise Park
Sunderland SR5 2TH
United Kingdom

Tel: +44 (0) 191 549 5002
Fax: +44 (0) 191 549 9005

E-mail: info@ciatraining.co.uk
Web: www.ciatraining.co.uk

ISBN-13: 978 1 86005 658 1

This training, which has been approved by ECDL Foundation, includes exercise items intended to assist Candidates in their training for an ECDL Certification Programme. These exercises are not ECDL Foundation certification tests. For information about authorised Test Centres in different national territories, please refer to the ECDL Foundation website at www.ecdl.org

First published 2009

Downloading the Data Files

The data associated with these exercises must be downloaded from our website. Go to: ***www.ciatraining.co.uk/data***. Follow the on screen instructions to download the appropriate data files.

By default, the data files will be downloaded to **My Documents\CIA DATA FILES\Advanced ECDL\AM6 PowerPoint 2003 Data**.

If you prefer, the data can be supplied on CD at an additional cost. Contact the Sales team at ***info@ciatraining.co.uk***.

Aims

To demonstrate the ability to use a presentation application on a personal computer.

To demonstrate some of the more advanced features using *PowerPoint.*

Objectives

After completing the guide the user will be able to:

- create and add slides of various kinds to a presentation
- change colour schemes and background effects
- use clip art and drawing tools
- manipulate images
- add animation, sound and video clips
- create and edit charts and flowcharts
- format text, bullets and fonts
- create links to other objects outside the presentation
- produce custom slide shows

Assessment of Knowledge

At the end of this guide is a section called the **Record of Achievement Matrix**. Before the guide is started it is recommended that the user completes the matrix to measure the level of current knowledge.

Tick boxes are provided for each feature. **1** is for no knowledge, **2** some knowledge and **3** is for competent.

After working through a section, complete the matrix for that section and only when competent in all areas move on to the next section.

Contents

Section 1 Preparation

By the end of this Section you should be able to:

Know how to Plan a Presentation

Consider how to Use Colour Schemes

Be Aware of Accessibility Issues

Use Background Colours and Effects

Bullet Levels

Create, Save and Use a Template

Work with Master Slides

Use A Word Processed Outline for Text

Insert Slides

To gain an understanding of the above features, work through the **Driving Lessons** in this **Section**.

For each **Driving Lesson**, read the **Park and Read** instructions, without touching the keyboard, then work through the numbered steps of the **Manoeuvres** on the computer. Complete the **Revision Exercise(s)** at the end of the section to test your knowledge.

Driving Lesson 1 - Design Considerations

Park and Read

PowerPoint is a powerful presentation graphics application, which allows impressive presentations to be produced with ease. Presentations can be viewed on screen, on an overhead projector, on 35mm slides, or as web pages.

Whilst this guide describes techniques needed to produce and run successful presentations, some thought should always be given to the target audience. Consider how to put your message across: the tone will need to be different for each audience, e.g. it would not be appropriate to deliver a presentation created for children to a business audience, or vice versa. You should also be aware of the level of knowledge the audience has of the subject and pitch the presentation accordingly. Too much explanation of areas with which the audience is familiar may cause them to lose interest. Likewise, too little explanation for an audience with little or no subject knowledge may have the same effect. Consider too the cultural background of the audience and make the presentation fit.

Practical considerations are also important. How big is the audience? How big is the room in which the presentation is to be delivered? Is the layout suitable - will everyone be able to see the presentation? Is the lighting adequate? You may need a projector and a microphone in a large room. Things like background colour and text legibility become more important in these circumstances.

Plan the length of the presentation appropriately. How much time is available? It may be necessary to create a long or short version of the slide show. Make sure the presentation makes sense and that the slides run in a logical manner. Set the slide timings appropriately; allow enough time to get the points across, but don't ramble or you may lose the attention of the audience.

Visual impact is almost everything in a presentation; the graphics and text support the dialogue. You should be aware of the value of using pictures rather than too much text and charts rather than rows of figures. At the same time, don't use too many different background colours or effects, or complicated detail; a consistent design scheme makes the message much clearer. Make sure the slides are clear with adequately contrasting colours.

These aesthetic, practical and ethical considerations should be at the forefront when designing any presentation.

Driving Lesson 2 - Colour Schemes and Accessibility

Park and Read

To some extent the final visual quality of a slide is a matter of opinion, but there are some guidelines which can be applied. Good use of contrast is important, but too much colour can distract the audience from the main focus of the slide. Avoid colour combinations that will make it difficult for people with colour blindness to see, i.e. red-green and blue-yellow.

There are other accessibility considerations, e.g. for anyone with visual impairment you may need to increase the size of fonts used. Indeed, for any audience limit the number of fonts used and remember that sans serif fonts are clearer and easier to read. Limit the number of animations and transitions used if you are presenting to an audience who may be visually impaired. Some people with cognitive or visual disabilities are unable to read moving text, or it can cause so much distraction that they are unable to read the rest of the page. Screen readers can't usually read moving text either.

Because of accessibility issues, a presentation may be intended to be viewed on the web. In this situation you must ensure alternative text is added to graphical objects, because if a screen reader is used, any image without alternative text will not be recognised.

It is normal practice to use **colour schemes** in slides. A colour scheme is a set of predetermined colours that is applied to specific areas of a slide. When a presentation is first created, a particular colour scheme is applied by default, but this scheme can be changed or a new one selected. Standard colour schemes are designed to compliment the design template of the presentation, but individual colours within a scheme can be amended.

Manoeuvres

1. Start *PowerPoint*, and from the **Open** area of the **Getting Started Task Pane** click More... . Open the presentation **Assessment** from the data files supplied with this course (see page 4 - **Downloading Data Files** for the location).
2. This presentation has a design template of **Artsy** applied. In **Normal View** the **Slides** pane shows the consistent appearance of the slides.
3. To change the colour scheme select **Format | Slide Design** and from the **Slide Design Task Pane** click Color Schemes . The scheme at the top left is the default scheme for this design.

Driving Lesson 2 - Continued

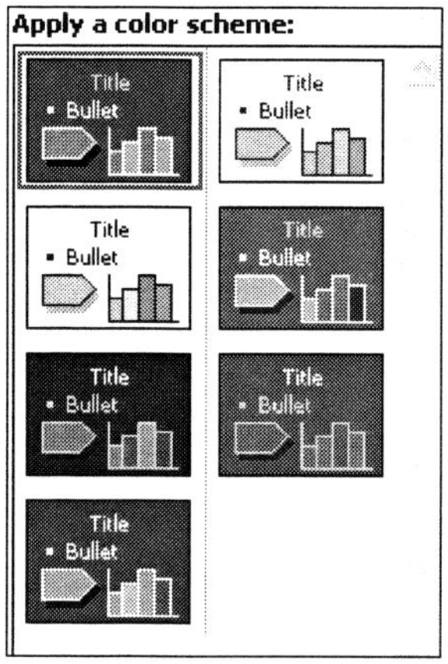

4. Click on the arrow at the right of the fifth scheme (with the dark red background) and select **Apply to All Slides**. All slides in the presentation change to the new colour scheme. The design template remains the same.

*The new scheme could be applied to the currently selected slide only by selecting the **Apply to Selected Slides** option. To maintain a consistent look to the presentation, however, it is recommended that all slides be changed.*

5. To customise the scheme click Edit Color Schemes... at the bottom of the **Task Pane**. A dialog box is displayed showing the individual colours that make up the current colour scheme.

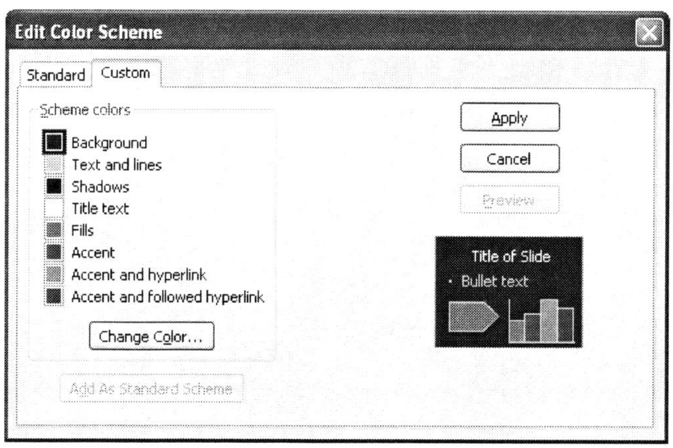

6. Select the small colour box for **Title text** and click **Change Color**. A colour chart is displayed showing the current colour for this feature.

Driving Lesson 2 - Continued

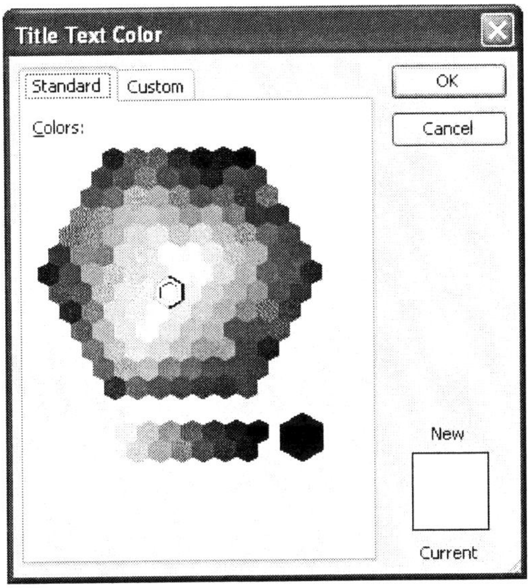

7. Select a pale pink colour from the chart and click **OK**.
8. The new colour for **Title text** is shown in the dialog box. Click **Apply** to change it on all of the slides.
9. Leave the presentation open for the next Driving Lesson.

Driving Lesson 3 - Background Effects

Park and Read

As well as colour changes, various other effects can be applied to the overall slide background. These can be applied to slides with or without design templates already in place, and generally they are more effective when applied to less cluttered slide designs. Effects that can be added are colour gradients, textures, patterns and pictures.

Manoeuvres

1. With the **Assessment** presentation open in **Normal** view select **Format | Background**.

2. To apply a background effect, click on the arrow of the drop down box to change the background colour and then select **Fill Effects**. Make sure the **Gradient** tab is selected.

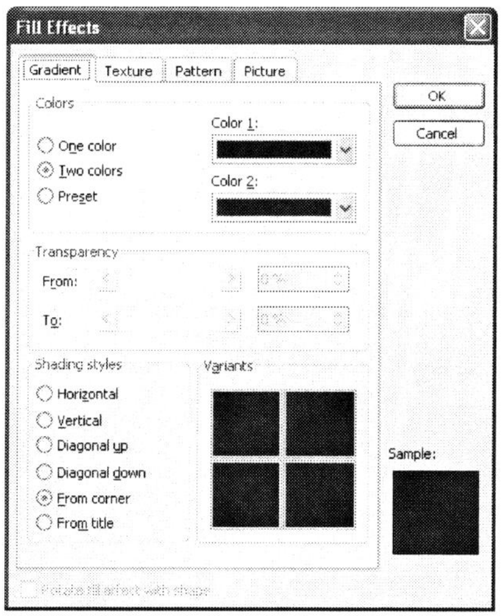

3. Colour gradients can be created from any two colours (**Color 1** and **Color 2**) or selected from an existing list. Click **Preset** and select **Late Sunset** from the drop down list.

4. Click **OK** then **Apply to All**.

Only the background of the slides changes. This can cause problems if a new background causes the content of the slides to be less visible, e.g. if a light background is applied behind light coloured text. Some trial and error may be involved to find a suitable effect.

Driving Lesson 3 - Continued

5. Select **Format | Background**, click the drop down arrow and select **Fill Effects**. This time select the **Texture** tab.
6. Click on each available texture - the name of each texture is displayed underneath.
7. Select **Brown marble**. Click **OK** then **Apply to All**.
8. Display the **Fill Effects** dialog box again and select the **Pattern** tab.
9. A selection of patterns is available based on a **Foreground** and **Background** colour (these can be changed). Select a reasonably dark pattern and click **OK**.
10. Click **Apply to All** to see the effect.
11. Display the **Fill Effects** dialog box again and select the **Picture** tab.
12. Any picture from the computer can be used as a background. Click **Select Picture** and ensure the supplied data folder is shown in the **Look in** box.
13. Select the **ostrich** file and click **Insert**. Click **OK**, then **Apply to All**.
14. With a picture background, existing graphics may not be appropriate. Select **Format | Background**.
15. Select the option to **Omit background graphics from master** from the **Background** dialog box. Click **Apply to All**.

Pictures can be effective backgrounds and add an exclusive appearance to a presentation, but care must be taken. Pictures are more likely to distract attention from the slide contents.

16. Save the presentation as **Big Bird** and close it.

Driving Lesson 4 - The Slide Master

Park and Read

Master pages contain text or graphics that are to be used on every page of a presentation. There are four master pages: **Slide**, **Title**, **Handout** and **Notes**.

The **Slide Master** allows uniform text or graphics to be added to every slide. A coloured or themed background may also be added. This will create a consistent look to the presentation.

Manoeuvres

1. Start a new, blank presentation. It should contain a single **Title Slide** with no data.

2. Select **View | Master | Slide Master**. The slide master is now shown.

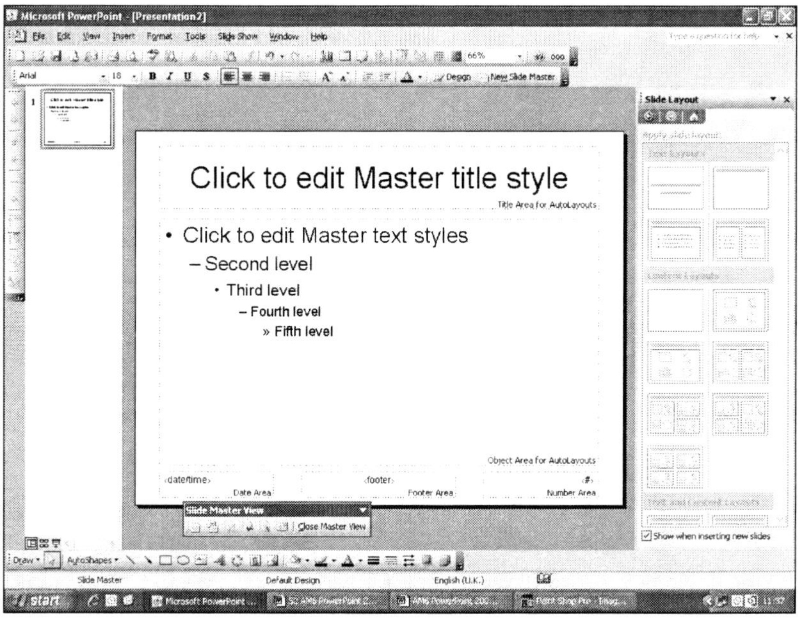

Any changes made in this view will affect the whole presentation and anything put on to this slide will appear on every slide.

3. Close the task pane and click on the text **Click to edit Master title style**.

Driving Lesson 4 - Continued

4. From the **Font** drop down list, 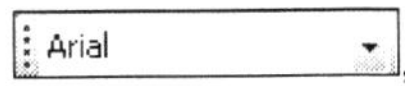, on the **Formatting** toolbar, select the **Arial Rounded MT Bold** font (use an alternative if this is unavailable).
5. Change the size to **48pt**.
6. Select the second text box: **Click to edit Master text styles**.
7. Click on the top bullet's text and select the font **Arial Rounded MT Bold** but leave the font size as **32pt**.

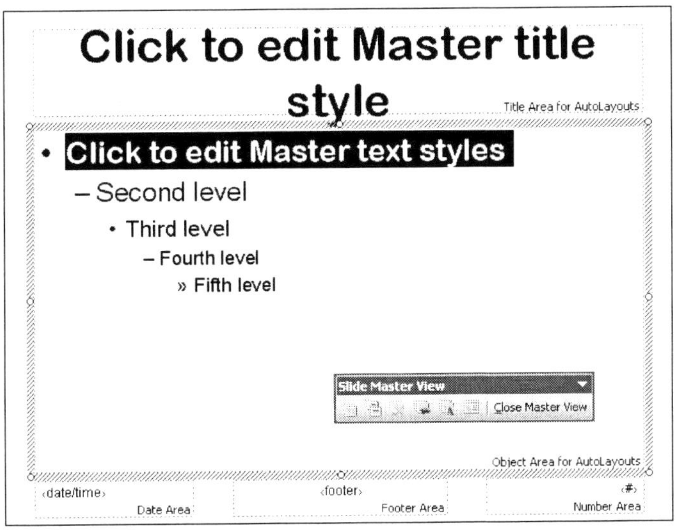

8. Click on the border of the **Footer Area** placeholder at the bottom of the slide master to select it and then press <**Delete**> to remove it.
9. Now click on the **Date Area** placeholder to select it and drag it to the centre position.
10. Select **Format | Background**. Click the drop down arrow in the dialog box and select **Fill Effects**. Make sure the **Gradient** tab is selected.
11. Apply a two colour gradient fill effect, using pale blue as **Color 1** and grey as **Color 2**, with a **Shading style** of **Diagonal up**, first variant. Click **OK**, then **Apply**.
12. Leave the slide master open.

Driving Lesson 5 - Bullet Levels

Park and Read

Bullets are used to emphasise points in a slide. They can have many different types of symbols. In **Slide Master View** there are several levels of bulleted text available. This allows minor details to be made about major points. By default the bullet levels use the same style of font, etc. but the style can be changed for each level.

Manoeuvres

1. The slide master should still be open. Notice that there are 5 bullet levels available.
2. Click in the **Second level bullet text** and change the font to **Arial Rounded MT Bold**. Apply an italic effect. Leave the font size the same.
3. To change the bullet character for the second level bullet, make sure the cursor is within the bullet text.
4. Select **Format | Bullets and Numbering**, **Bulleted** tab and select the third style on the bottom row of the dialog box.

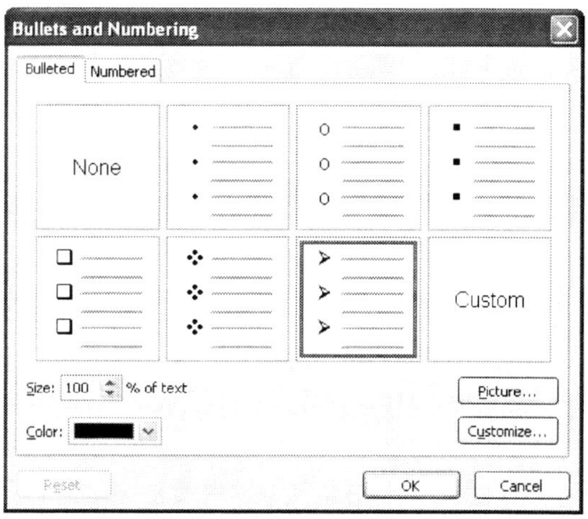

5. Click **OK** to apply the new bullet character.
6. Click in the **Third level bullet text** and change the font to **Arial Rounded MT Bold**, leave the size as **24pt**.
7. Display the **Bullets and Numbering** dialog box and ensure the bullet character is the first style (not **None**) on the top row. Click **OK**.
8. Leave the slide master open and move on to the next Driving Lesson.

Driving Lesson 6 - The Title Master

Park and Read

Unlike the slide master, the **title master** only affects the **Title Slide**. It allows you to create a different look for your opening slide in your presentation, or for any slides that may be used to introduce a new section in the presentation.

The slide master should be created first before changing the title master, as any formatting which is changed on the slide master also changes the title master.

Manoeuvres

1. The slide master should still be open, click the **Insert New Title Master** button, , on the **Slide Master View** toolbar. The title master is shown.

2. Click on the text **Click to edit Master title style** and change the font to **Broadway** (or some other distinctive font if this is unavailable).
3. Change the font size to **50pt** (you will need to type the size into the box and press <**Enter**>).
4. Click on the text **Click to edit Master subtitle style** and change the font to **Tahoma**.
5. Change the font size to **36pt** and close **Master View**.
6. Insert 3 new **Title and Text** slides.

Driving Lesson 6 - Continued

7. So you can identify the slides, add a title of **Title Slide** to the first slide, **Slide 2** to the second slide, **Slide 3** to the third slide and **Slide 4** to the fourth slide. Notice the different fonts on the slides as defined by the master slides.

8. Custom slide masters can be added. Return to **Slide Master View** and insert a new slide master by clicking **Insert New Slide Master**, 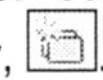.

9. This master is to be used by specific slides only. Apply the same fonts as on the default slide master, but make the background pale green.

10. To apply this custom slide master to slide **4** only, close **Master View**. Right click on slide **4**'s icon in the **Slides** pane and select **Slide Design** from the shortcut menu.

11. In the **Slide Design** task pane, there is now an icon for each slide master in this presentation.

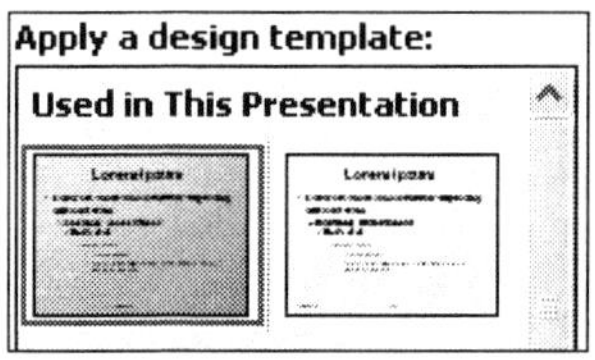

12. Click on the drop down arrow at the right of the green **Custom Design** slide.

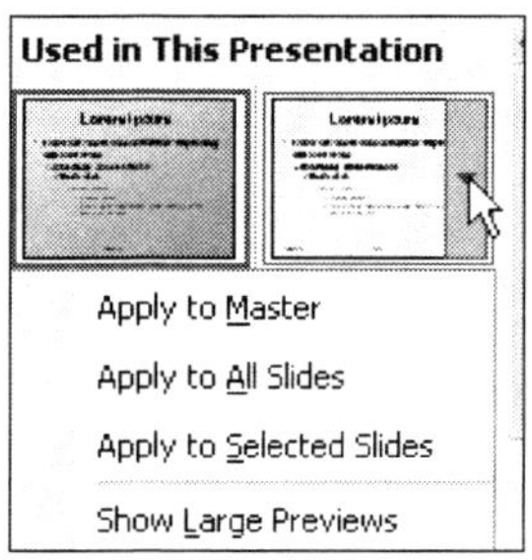

13. Select **Apply to Selected Slides** from the menu.

14. Click on each slide in turn in the **Slides** pane. Slide **1** has the **Title Master** applied, slides **2** and **3** the default slide master and slide **4** the custom slide master.

15. Insert a new **Title and Text** slide at the end of the presentation. The green slide master is applied, as it was the last design used. Change the design to the default master for the new slide.

16. Save the presentation as **Custom Masters** and close it.

Driving Lesson 7 - Creating a Template

Park and Read

Having spent considerable time and effort creating a suitable appearance for your presentation, you may wish to apply the same look to subsequent slide shows. Any layout can be saved as a **template** and then used as a basis for further presentations. This is particularly relevant for organisations, which often want a consistent corporate image for all their presentations.

Templates often contain only suitably formatted master slides so that any content can be added to create a presentation.

Manoeuvres

1. Create a new blank presentation with an empty **Title Slide**.
2. To create the template's style and background, first select **Format | Slide Design** and apply the design template **Blends** from the **Task Pane**.
3. Select **View | Master | Slide Master**. Applying the design template has created a **Slide Master** and a **Title Master** as shown on the left of the screen.
4. Click on the master number **1**, the **Slide Master** (master number **2** is the **Title Master**).
5. Select **Format | Background** and display the **Fill Effects** dialog box.
6. Select the **Texture** tab then scroll down and select the texture **Papyrus**. Click **OK** then **Apply to All**. The background is applied to both masters.

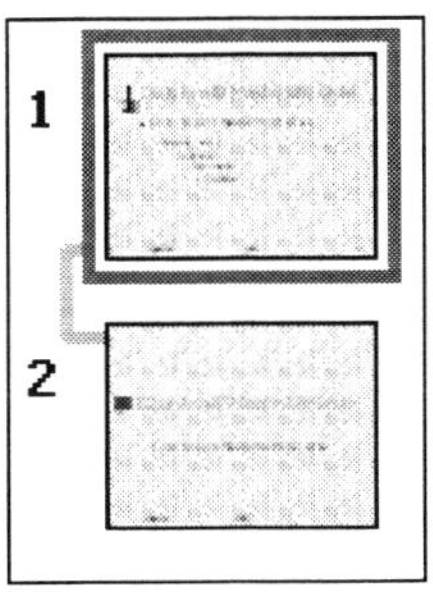

7. Click in the **Master title style** area and change the style to italic.
8. Click on the first bullet line and select **Format | Bullets and Numbering**.

Driving Lesson 7 - Continued

9. Select an arrow style bullet, ➢ and click **OK**. With the cursor still in the first line, select **Format | Line Spacing** and enter a **Line spacing** of **2** lines. Click **OK**.

10. Select **Insert | Picture | From File** or click from the **Drawing** toolbar, and insert the picture **safari.gif** from the supplied data files as a logo. Drag the picture to the lower right corner of the **Object Area**.

11. Close **Master View**. The layout of the slide is now ready to be saved as a template so that it can be easily used for other presentations. Select **File | Save As**.

12. In the **Save As** dialog box make sure the **File name** is **Example** and select **Design Template (*.pot)** from **Save as type**. When this file type is selected the **Save in** box will automatically show **Templates**, the location of the existing *PowerPoint* templates. Click the **Save** button, Save.

Templates could be stored in any location but would not then be automatically available within PowerPoint.

13. Select **File | Close** to close the presentation.

14. Reopen the **Example** template, using the list of files at the bottom of the **File** menu.

15. Switch to **Master View** and change the texture of the **Slide Master** to **Canvas**.

16. Close **Master View** then use the **Save** button to save the template.

17. Close the presentation.

Driving Lesson 8 - Using a Template

Park and Read

Once a template has been saved it can be used to set the appearance of future presentations. New presentations can be started with the design template or existing slides can be converted.

Manoeuvres

1. Select **File | New**. As the **Example** template created in the last was saved in the **Templates** folder, it can now be accessed from the **Templates** area of the **Task Pane**. Click 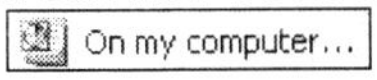 and ensure the **General** tab is selected.

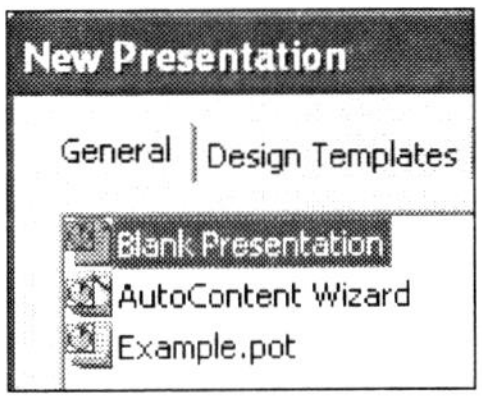

2. Select **Example** and click **OK**. On the blank title slide, enter **Example** as the title text and your organisation name as the subtitle text.
3. Click  , to insert a new slide and select the **Title and Text** layout.
4. Click to add a title of **Contents** and add two bulleted text lines of **Introduction** and **History**. Notice that all of the features defined when creating the template are being applied here, e.g. background, title style, bullet style, line spacing, logo.

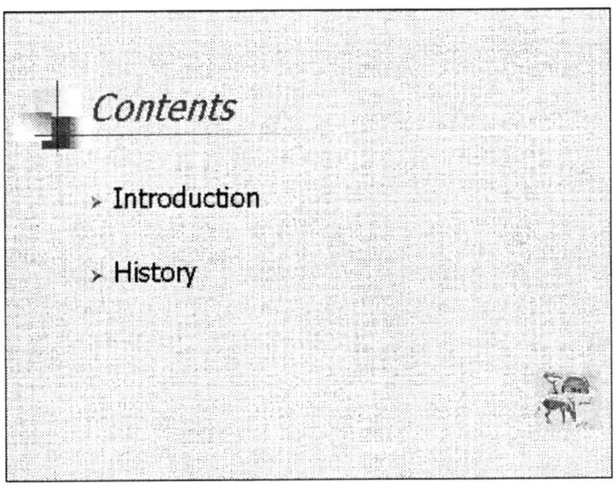

Driving Lesson 8 - Continued

5. Close the new presentation without saving and open the presentation **Assessment** from the supplied data files.

6. To apply the layout and colours of the template select **Format | Slide Design**.

7. Click Browse... at the bottom of the **Task Pane**.

8. The new template **Example** should now be available from the dialog box. Select it and click **Apply**.

9. All features of the layout are applied to all of the slides in the presentation. Display slide 2 in **Normal View** to see the effect more clearly.

Because the template is applied after the slides have been created there may be some conflict, e.g. Slide 4. It is usually better to start with the desired design and compose the slide contents to fit.

10. To delete a template, click Browse... again and right click on the **Example** template.

11. Select **Delete** from the shortcut menu. Click **Yes** at the confirmation dialog box and the template is deleted.

12. Close the dialog box.

Any existing slides based on the template will not be affected.

13. Close the presentation without saving.

Driving Lesson 9 - Inserting Text

Park and Read

Individual sections of text can be imported into a *PowerPoint* presentation from word processing applications by using **Copy** and **Paste**. However, if a document is created with the correct styles already set up, it can be imported using a menu command in *PowerPoint* and will create new slides directly.

Manoeuvres

1. Open the word processing application *Word* and open the file **induction.doc**, which is included with the supplied *PowerPoint* files.
2. Make sure **Outline View**, , is selected. The text; has been formatted at different levels. When imported into *PowerPoint*, the highest level will be become slide titles, the next level 1st level bullet points, and so on.
3. Close the document and close *Word*.
4. In *PowerPoint* create a new blank presentation. On the **Title Slide**, add **Induction** as the title text and your organisation name as the subtitle text.
5. Apply a design template of **Globe** from the **Slide Design Task Pane**.
6. To import the outline select **Insert | Slides from Outline**. Locate the supplied data folder and select **All Outlines** from **Files of type**.

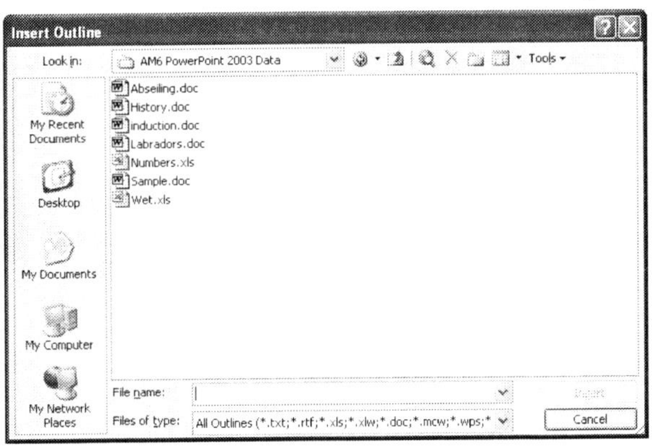

7. Select the file **induction** and click the **Insert** button, Insert.

There may be a message about installing new features. Click ***No****.*

8. Three new slides are created from the outline file, look at the **Slides** pane to see them all. Compare their structure with the original file layout.
9. Save the presentation as **Induction** and leave it open.

Driving Lesson 10 - Inserting Slides

Park and Read

Slides from existing presentations or even whole presentations, can be imported into the current presentation.

Manoeuvres

1. View the **Induction** presentation in **Normal View** and select slide **4**, **Health and Safety**, from the **Slides** pane.
2. To import a slide, select **Insert | Slides from Files** to display the **Slide Finder** dialog box.
3. Click the **Browse** button and select the location of the data files from the **Look in** area of the **Browse** dialog box.
4. Select the **Seminar** presentation and click **Open**. The **Slide Finder** dialog box appears with the slides from the selected presentation shown in the **Select slides** area. Click on slide **3**, **The Company**.

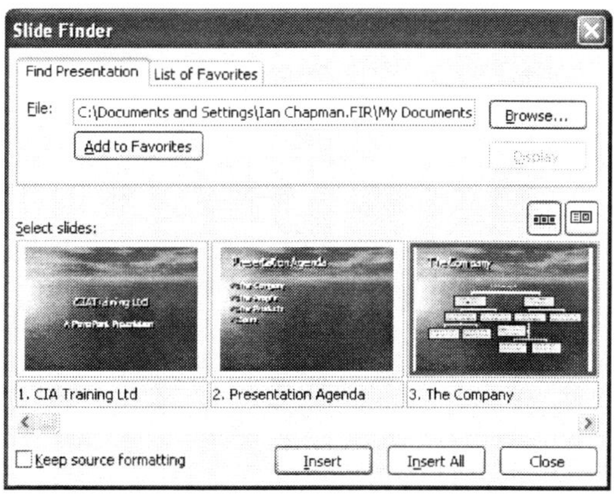

5. Click the **Insert** button to place the slide into the **Induction** presentation. There may be a delay as the slide is changed to match the design of the **Induction** presentation.
6. To insert more slides from a different presentation click **Browse** on the **Slide Finder** dialog box (it should still be displayed). Select the **Extras** presentation and click **Open**.
7. Click **Insert All** to place all four slides of this presentation into **Induction**.
8. Close the **Slide Finder** dialog box and view all nine slides in the **Induction** presentation.
9. Save the presentation and close it.

Driving Lesson 11 - Revision

This is not an ECDL test. Testing may only be carried out through certified ECDL test centres. This covers the features introduced in this section. Try not to refer to the preceding Driving Lessons while completing it.

1. After a presentation has been created, name 4 ways to present the final show.
2. Is it good practice to give the same presentations to all audiences - why?
3. What effect might slides with lots of different colours have on an audience?
4. Why should care be taken when choosing colour combinations?
5. What type of background effects can be applied to slides?
6. Create a new blank presentation, add a title of **Tours** to the default title slide and apply a **Design Template** of **Ocean**.
7. Use **Insert | Slides from Outline** to create slides from the document **History**. The document is already in the correct format.
8. Add another slide at the end of the presentation by inserting slide **7** from the **Assessment** presentation. Is it necessary to change the design of the inserted slide?
9. Save the presentation as **Tours** and close it.

Check the answers at the back of the guide.

If you experienced any difficulty completing this Revision refer back to the Driving Lessons in this section. Then redo the Revision.

Driving Lesson 12 - Revision

This is not an ECDL test. Testing may only be carried out through certified ECDL test centres. This covers the features introduced in this section. Try not to refer to the preceding Driving Lessons while completing it.

1. Open the presentation **Kittens**.
2. Apply a colour scheme. Select the fourth scheme (with the pale coloured background) and click **Edit Color Schemes** to customise it.
3. Change the colour of the scheme's **Title text** to dark brown and apply the scheme.
4. Change the background of all slides to a **Texture** effect of **White marble**.
5. Save the presentation as **Background** and close it.
6. Start a new, blank presentation. A template is to be created.
7. View the slide master and change the font of the **Title text**, **Master text style** and **Second level** text to **Tahoma**.
8. Apply a two colour gradient background effect with colour 1 as olive green and colour 2 as a light green. Apply to all slides.
9. Close **Master View** then save as a template named **Gradient** and close it.
10. Use the template to create the following slides:

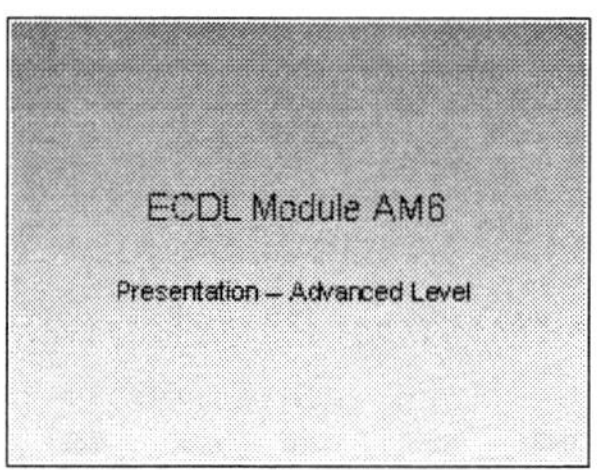

1

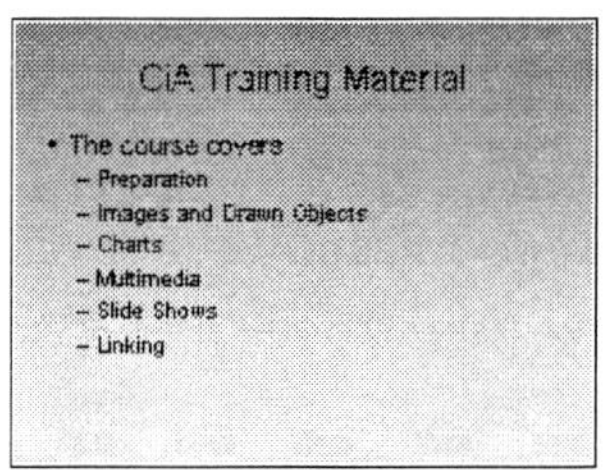

2

*You will need to demote the bullet points making up the list on slide **2** using the **Demote** button, [icon], on the **Outlining** toolbar.*

11. Save the presentation as **AM6** and close it. Delete the **Gradient** template.

If you experienced any difficulty completing this Revision refer back to the Driving Lessons in this section. Then redo the Revision.

Once you are confident with the features, complete the Record of Achievement Matrix referring to the section at the end of the guide. Only when competent move on to the next Section.

Section 2 Images & Drawn Objects

By the end of this Section you should be able to:

Work with Drawn Objects

Change Object Backgrounds

Rotate and Flip Images

Select and Manipulate Multiple Objects

Recolour Pictures

Crop and Edit Images

Save Images in Different File Formats

To gain an understanding of the above features, work through the **Driving Lessons** in this **Section**.

For each **Driving Lesson**, read the **Park and Read** instructions, without touching the keyboard, then work through the numbered steps of the **Manoeuvres** on the computer. Complete the **Revision Exercise(s)** at the end of the section to test your knowledge.

Driving Lesson 13 - Drawing Objects

Park and Read

The **Drawing** toolbar allows drawings to be made directly on to a slide. The **Drawing** toolbar can only be displayed in **Normal** and **Notes Pages View**. Some of the buttons for drawing objects are:

Select Objects	Insert WordArt
AutoShapes	Fill Color
Line	Line Color
Arrow	Font Color
Rectangle	Line Style
Oval	Dash Style
Text box	Arrow Style
3D Style	Shadow Style

Objects can be drawn by clicking on the appropriate button and then clicking and dragging on the slide. All objects have **handles**, similar to clip art, that can be used to reshape and re-size the drawing. Once drawn, objects can have various effects applied to them.

Manoeuvres

1. Start a new blank presentation and create a new, **Title Only**, slide and enter the title **Drawing**.
2. If the **Drawing** toolbar is not already on view (usually along the lower edge of the display), select **View | Toolbars | Drawing** to display it.
3. Use the appropriate tool to draw a rectangle anywhere on the slide.
4. To change its colour click the drop down arrow on the **Fill Color** button, and then click on one of the available colours. It is immediately applied to the rectangle.
5. Move the coloured rectangle until it obscures the slide title.

Driving Lesson 13 - Continued

6. With the rectangle still selected (handles visible), click on the drop down arrow on the **Fill Color** button and select **More Fill Colors**.

7. Select a red colour from the grid and drag the **Transparency** slider to the right until **80%** is shown in the box.

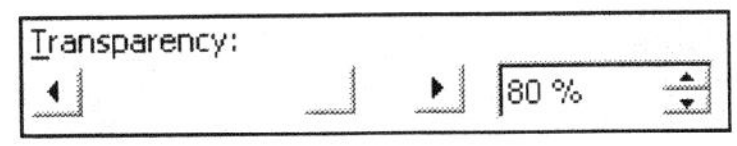

8. Click **OK** to apply the effect. The title can now be seen behind the rectangle.

9. Drag the rectangle away from the title, click on the drop down arrow on the **Fill Color** button and select **More Fill Colors**.

10. Leave the colour as it is but change the figure in the **Transparency** box to **0**. Click **OK**.

11. To apply a 3-D effect, with the rectangle still selected (handles visible) click the **3-D Style** button,  on the **Drawing** toolbar.

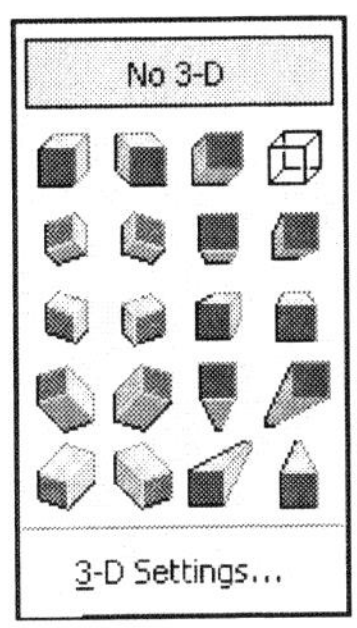

12. Click the first style and the effect is applied to the rectangle immediately.

13. Click the **3-D Style** button again and select **3-D Settings**. A toolbar is displayed with options to alter the 3-D effects.

14. Click the drop down arrow on the **3-D Color** button, , and select a dark blue colour (select **More 3-D Colors** first if necessary). The colour of the 3-D part of the shape is altered.

15. Click the **Surface** button, , and select the **Wire Frame** option. The rectangle is seen only as a frame.

16. Try some of the other effects on the **3-D Settings** toolbar.

17. Click the **3-D** button and select **No 3-D**. The rectangle is returned to its original form.

18. Close the **3-D Settings** toolbar.

19. Leave the slide open for the next Driving Lesson.

Driving Lesson 14 - Object Backgrounds

Park and Read

The range of background options available to slides can also be applied to drawn objects.

Manoeuvres

1. Select the rectangle drawn in the previous Driving Lesson. To apply an effect click the drop down arrow on the **Fill Color** button,  and choose **Fill Effects** from the shortcut menu.

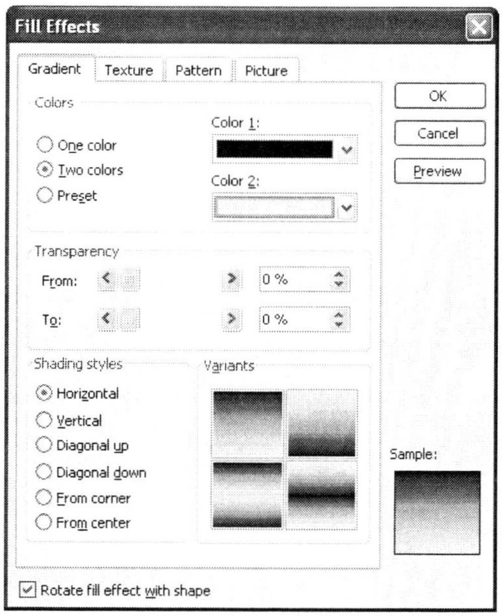

2. Under the **Gradient** tab, try changing the options for **Colors** and **Shading styles** and see the various effects shown in the **Sample** box. Do not click **OK**.
3. Finally select the **Two colors** option and a **Shading style** of **Horizontal shading**.
4. Select a dark blue colour for **Color 1** and a lighter blue for **Color 2**.
5. Click **OK** to see the effect on the rectangle.
6. Draw an oval shape next to the rectangle, click on the drop down arrow on the **Fill Color** button, and choose **Fill Effects** from the shortcut menu.
7. Select the **Texture** tab and click on the first texture, **Newsprint**. Click **OK** to see the effect on the drawn oval.
8. Use **AutoShapes | Basic Shapes** to draw a triangle next to the oval. Click on the drop down arrow on the **Fill Color** button, and choose **Fill Effects**.
9. Select the **Pattern** tab and click on the **Horizontal brick** pattern. Select contrasting dark and light colours for the **Foreground** and **Background**.

Driving Lesson 14 - Continued

10. Click **OK** to see the effect in the drawn triangle.
11. Resize and move the shapes until the slide is similar to the picture below.

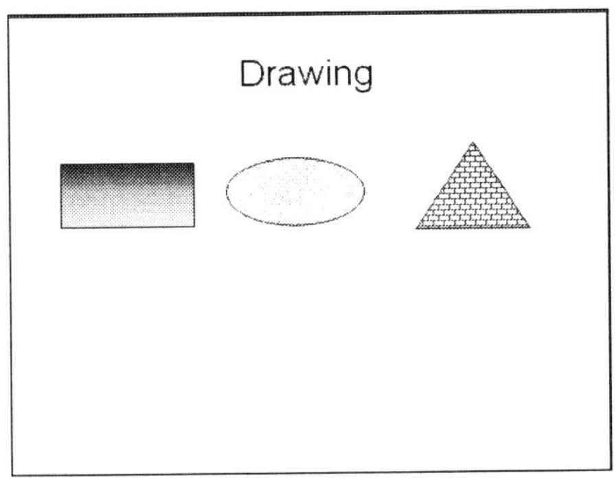

12. Select the triangle.
13. To apply the same formatting to the oval, with the triangle selected click the **Format Painter** button, .
14. Now click on the oval. Click **Undo** to return the oval to its original colours.

*To apply the same formatting to several objects, double click , then click on each object in turn. Click the button again, or press <**Esc**> to end the formatting.*

15. Right click on the rectangle. To make this fill effect the default formatting for all new objects, select **Set AutoShape Defaults**.
16. Draw any shape in the middle of the slide. The rectangle's formatting is now automatically applied to all new objects within this presentation.
17. Click on the last shape you've drawn and press <**Delete**> to remove it.
18. Draw a heart (from **Basic Shapes**) beneath the oval and select **Format | Autoshape**. Select the drop down arrow on the **Fill Color** box and select **Fill Effects**. This is an alternative way to display the **Fill Effects** dialog box.
19. From the **Picture** tab, click **Select Picture** and select the **canyon** image from the data files.
20. Click **Insert** and then **OK** to apply a picture fill to the heart.
21. Delete the heart using the <**Delete**> key and leave the slide open for the next Driving Lesson.

*You may to change the **AutoShape Default** effect now by filling another shape with a simple fill colour and setting that as the default.*

Driving Lesson 15 - Rotating or Flipping Objects

Park and Read

Any drawn object can be rotated or flipped. Objects on a slide can be manipulated individually or several at a time.

Manoeuvres

1. Click on the rectangle to select it.
2. Move the mouse pointer over the green rotate handle of the object and click and drag. The rectangle is rotated about its centre.
3. Try rotating the object whilst holding down <**Shift**>. The object is rotated by 15° intervals rather than continuously.
4. Try rotating the object whilst holding down <**Ctrl**>. The object is rotated about one of its other handles.
5. Select the triangle.
6. Select **Draw | Rotate or Flip | Rotate Right 90^{0}**.

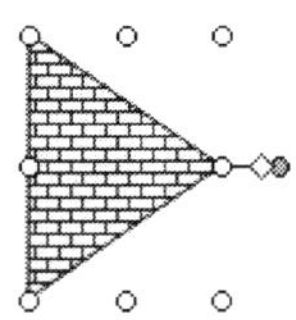

7. The triangle is rotated 90 degrees to the right. Select **Draw | Rotate or Flip | Rotate Right 90^{0}** again, the triangle will now be completely inverted.
8. Select **Draw | Rotate or Flip | Flip Vertical**. The triangle is now flipped over in a vertical direction so that it is now the original way up.
9. Try rotating and flipping the other objects.

Flipping regular shapes like rectangles may not produce a visible effect. Try rotating the shapes slightly before flipping them.

10. Return the objects to their starting orientation.
11. Select **Insert | Picture | From File** (or use the button) and insert the **Earlybird** image from the supplied data files onto the **Drawing** slide underneath the rectangle.

Driving Lesson 15 - Continued

12. Click to select the rectangle. Hold <**Shift**> down and select the oval and the image. All three objects should now be selected objects. Any formatting will now be applied to all objects.

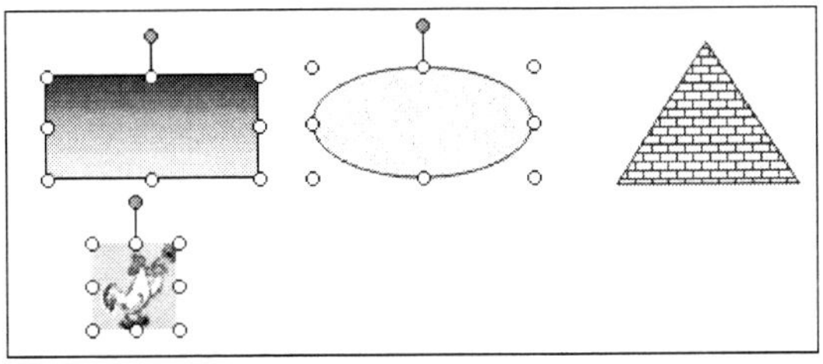

13. Click one of the corner handles of the rectangle and drag it slightly outwards to enlarge the object. All the selected objects will be enlarged by the same amount. Click away to deselect them.

14. Click the **Select Objects** button, . Click and drag around the three drawn objects. A dotted rectangle appears until the mouse button is released. Any shapes wholly within the rectangle will be selected.

15. Click on one of the selected shapes and move it slightly. All selected shapes will move in the same way. Click away to deselect them.

16. Arrange all objects on the slide in roughly the positions shown below.

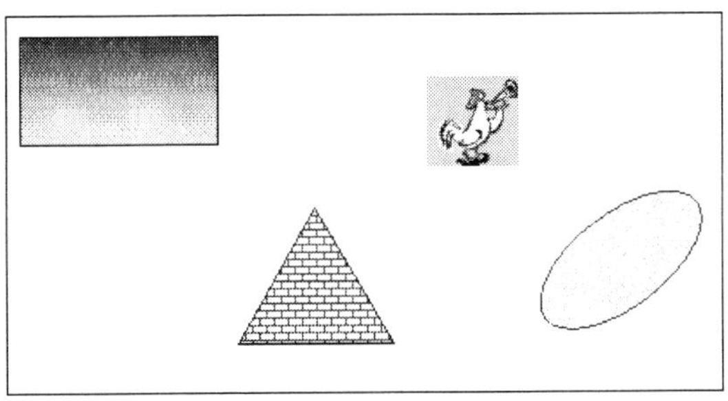

17. Save the presentation as **Shapes** and close it.

Driving Lesson 16 - Recolouring Pictures

Park and Read

Various types of picture or drawn image can be added to a presentation and may then have background effects applied. It is also possible to recolour a picture; you may wish to do this so that it matches the theme/design template more closely.

Manoeuvres

1. Open the presentation **Theatre**.
2. View slide **3** in **Normal View**. The graphic on this slide matches the colour scheme quite well.
3. Check slide **4**; this graphic is OK too.
4. Move to slide **5**. This image is not really a match for the scheme.
5. Right click on the picture and select **Format Picture** from the shortcut menu.
6. From the **Picture** tab, click the Recolor... button.

*Alternatively, click the **Recolor Picture** button, on the **Picture** toolbar.*

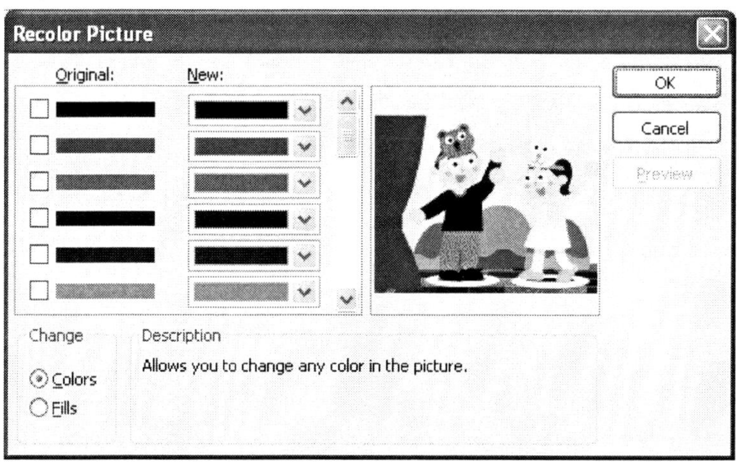

7. Scroll down the list of available colours and click in the box at the left of each pink or red shade to select it.
8. Scroll down until you can see the first checked box.

Driving Lesson 16 - Continued

9. Click on the drop down arrow next to **New** and choose a colour from the current scheme.

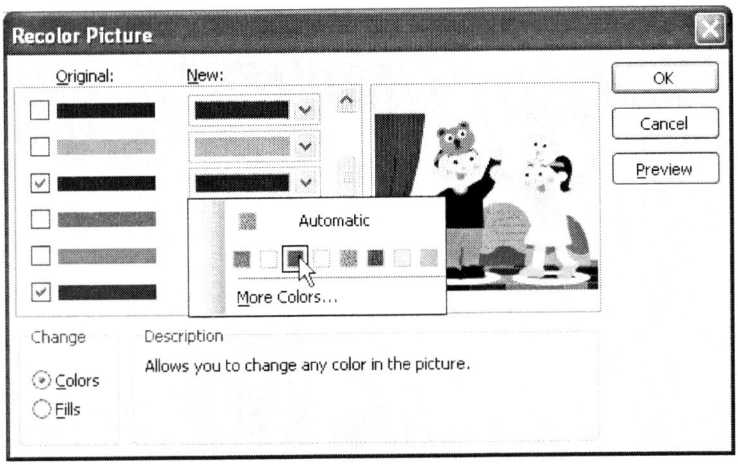

10. Repeat this for each checked colour and watch the preview change.

11. Click **OK** when all the colours have been changed to your satisfaction.

12. Click **OK** again.

13. With the picture still selected, click the **Reset Picture** button , on the **Picture** toolbar. All colours (and any size changes) will be restored to their original values.

14. Save the presentation as **Theatre2** and close it.

Driving Lesson 17 - Converting Pictures

Park and Read

Sometimes, before a picture can be manipulated, it must be converted to a drawn object, which means that its components are separated. You may need to do this if you want to recolour a particular area of a picture not available from the **Recolor Picture** dialog box. More can be done to change and enhance drawn objects than can be done to pictures.

Manoeuvres

1. Open the **Shapes** presentation which was saved earlier, insert the **Clip Art** image opposite using the search **backpacker** and move it away from the other objects.
2. The colour of the blue rucksack can only be changed if the picture is converted. To convert the image, right click on it and select **Grouping | Ungroup**. The following prompt appears:

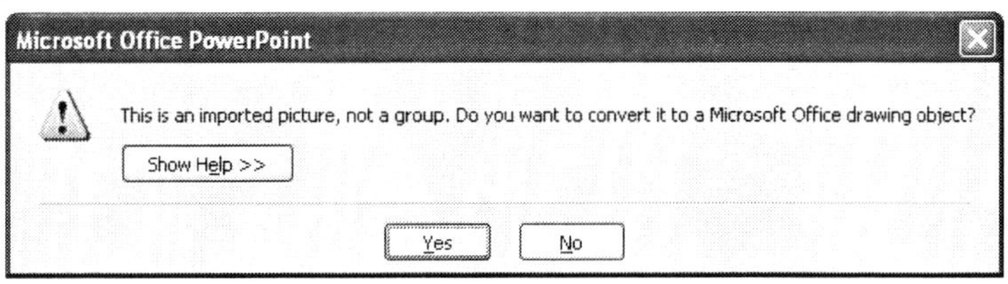

3. Click **Yes** to convert the picture. All component parts of the image are separated, or **ungrouped**. Click on the blue rucksack.

4. Notice the small handles around it. Change the fill colour to yellow.
5. Click away from the image. Click once on it to select it.

If you wanted to change the colours further, just click on the relevant part of the picture.

6. Leave the presentation open.

Driving Lesson 18 - Background Graphics

Park and Read

Graphics can be placed on the background of a slide using the **Slide Master**. However, this means that all slides would display the graphic. To apply a graphic to certain slides only, a setting must be applied to those slides on which the background graphics are <u>not</u> to appear.

Manoeuvres

1. Using the current presentation insert three new **Title Only** slides.
2. Name them **Slide 2**, **Slide 3** and **Slide 4**.
3. Select **View | Master | Slide Master** and insert the **freefall** image from the data files.
4. Drag the image to the bottom right corner and return to **Normal View**.
5. Move to slide **2** and select **Format | Background**.
6. To stop the image appearing on this slide check **Omit background graphics from master**.

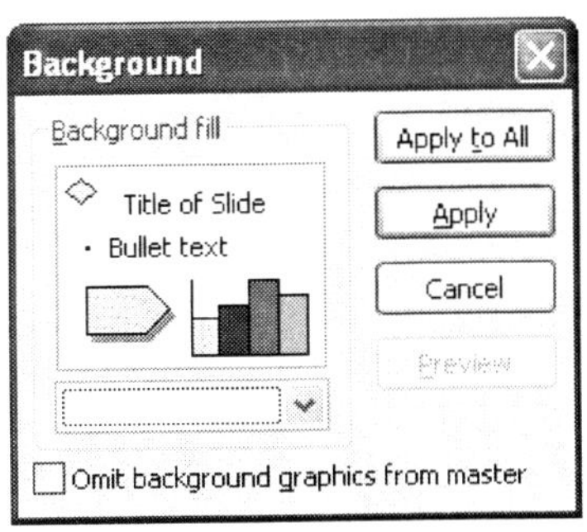

7. Click **Apply**.
8. Select slide **4** and repeat steps **5** to **7**.
9. Move to slide **1**. The graphic is displayed.
10. Note in the **Slides** pane that only slides **1** and **3** have the graphic, because it was omitted from the other slides.
11. Delete the graphic from the **Slide Master**.
12. Delete slides **2**, **3** and **4**.
13. Leave the presentation open for the next Driving Lesson.

Driving Lesson 19 - Arranging Objects

Park and Read

Individual objects can be moved and resized by clicking and dragging, but there are also commands available to align and position them with more accuracy. A grid and ruler can be displayed to assist when moving objects around.

Manoeuvres

1. The ruler and grids need to be displayed. Select **View | Ruler** and then select **View | Grid and Guides**.
2. The **Snap objects to grid** option automatically aligns objects with horizontal and vertical gridlines on the slide. Make sure this option is checked.
3. Click the drop down arrow in the **Spacing** box and select **2 grids per cm**. This produces a spacing of **0.5cm**.
4. Check **Display grid on screen**.

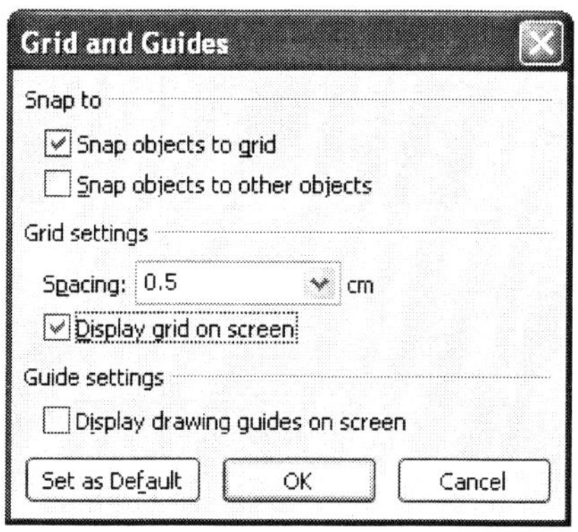

5. Click **OK** to apply the settings.
6. Slowly drag the rectangle around the slide; notice how it "jumps" when near a gridline (you may need to zoom in to see this properly).
7. Select **View | Grid and Guides** and remove the check from **Snap objects to grid**. Click **OK**.
8. Move the rectangle again and notice how it doesn't jump now.
9. Reapply snap to grid, but uncheck **Display grid on screen** and change **Spacing** to **5 grids per cm**. Click **OK**.

Driving Lesson 19 - Continued

10. In the **Grid and Guides** dialog box, select the option to **Display drawing guides on screen**, then click **OK**. A horizontal and a vertical guide are displayed which divide the slide into four areas for layout purposes.

11. Click and drag the vertical guide a few centimetres to the left and the a few centimetres horizontal guide a few centimetres downwards. The new layout will be available on all slides in the presentation.

12. Select **View | Grid and Guides** and remove the check from **Display drawing guides on screen**. Click **OK**.

13. Select **View | Ruler** again to hide the rulers.

14. Shapes can be positioned more exactly on the slide. Click on the rectangle. To specify its position select **Format | AutoShape** and select the **Position** tab from the dialog box.

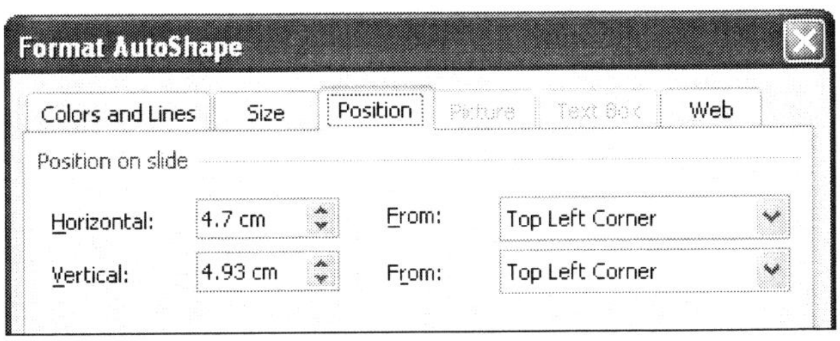

15. Set the **Horizontal** position to **2.0 cm** and the **Vertical** position to **10.0 cm**. Click **OK** and the rectangle will be positioned exactly at that location.

16. Use any method to select any four of the objects, including one of the pictures.

17. Select **Draw | Align or Distribute**. Make sure **Relative to Slide** is checked.

18. Select **Align Bottom** from the **Draw | Align or Distribute** menu. The objects are aligned with the bottom edge of the slide.

19. Select **Draw | Align or Distribute | Distribute Horizontally**. The objects will now be evenly spaced across the slide.

20. For the same objects apply **Align Left**, then **Distribute Vertically**.

*If **Relative to Slide** was not selected, the objects would be aligned and distributed only within the object group itself.*

21. Practise using the different aligning and distributing options within **Draw | Align or Distribute** to rearrange different groups of objects. Notice the difference when the **Relative to Slide** option is not selected.

22. Leave the presentation open for the next Driving Lesson.

Driving Lesson 20 - Cropping Images

Park and Read

Whilst many of the same features can be applied to images and to drawn objects, there are some processes which can only be applied to images. One of these is **cropping**, when only a selected part of the image is required. The original image is still available.

Manoeuvres

1. With the presentation from the last still open, create a new, **Title Only**, slide and enter the title **Image**.
2. Select **Insert | Picture | From File** and insert the image **ostrich** from the supplied data files.
3. Click and drag the image to the lower left area of the slide. Click on the top right handle around the image and drag it diagonally up and right to enlarge the picture. Dragging a corner handle to enlarge an image maintains its correct proportions.
4. If the **Picture** toolbar is not already on screen, select **View | Toolbars | Picture**. You need to crop the image so that only the head of the ostrich is displayed.
5. With the picture selected, click the **Crop** button, , on the **Picture** toolbar.
6. The picture is now surrounded by a cropping border and the mouse pointer changes. Move this pointer over the middle handle on the right edge of the image, and move it inwards. Release the mouse button. The picture will now be cropped.
7. Move the pointer over the middle handle on the lower edge of the image and drag it upwards, to crop the lower part of the picture.
8. Practise the cropping technique (the handles can be dragged outwards to reveal more of the picture if necessary) until only the head is displayed.

9. Click away from the image to remove the cropping cursor.
10. Leave the presentation open for the next Driving Lesson.

Driving Lesson 21 - Editing Images

Park and Read

There are many commands on the **Picture** toolbar that can be used to alter the appearance of images on slides.

Manoeuvres

1. To return the cropped image from the last to its original size and content, select it and click the **Reset Picture** button, , on the **Picture** toolbar.
2. Click and drag a corner handle to resize the image to about half the size of the slide.
3. Right click on the image and select **Format Picture**, then the **Size** tab.
4. Notice how **Lock aspect ratio** is checked. This means that when **Height** and **Width** settings from **Scale** are changed, they change in relation to each other to maintain the proportions of the image.

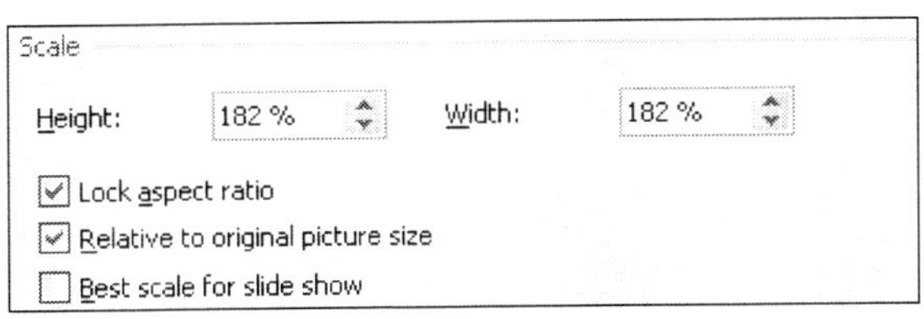

5. Change **Height** to **100%** and notice that **Width** changes at the same time.
6. Click **OK** to see how the image has been rescaled.
7. Display the **Format Picture** dialog box again and the **Size** tab. Uncheck **Lock aspect ratio**.
8. Change **Height** to **60%** and click **OK**. The image is now squashed, because it's been rescaled disproportionately.
9. Reset the picture.
10. Click the **Color** button, , on the **Picture** toolbar. Select **Grayscale** from the list of options.
11. The image changes to the appearance of a monochrome photograph.

Driving Lesson 21 - Continued

12. Click the **Color** button again and select **Black & White** to see the image in only those two shades.
13. Click the **Color** button again and select **Automatic** to return the image to its original colours.
14. Click the **Color** button again and select **Washout** to display the image as a watermark, which can then be used as a slide background for example.
15. Click the **Format Picture** button, , from the **Picture** toolbar. The **Format Picture** dialog box is displayed.

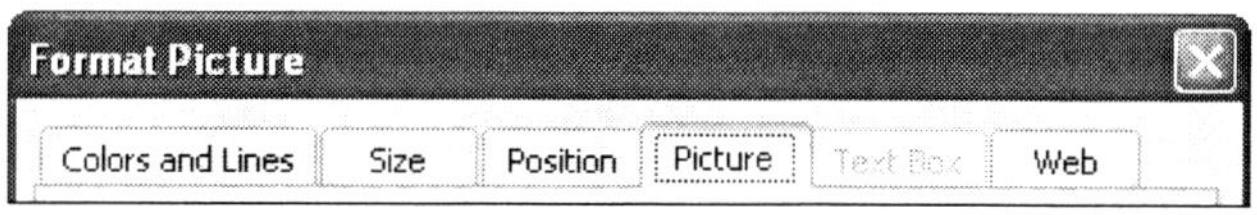

16. Many image formatting operations can be controlled from this dialog box. **Colors and Lines** allows borders to be drawn around the image; **Size** allows the precise size of the image to be defined as a percentage of the original dimensions; **Picture** allows cropping and watermarks to be defined numerically. Examine the available options on each of the tabs and try changing some of the settings to see the effect.
17. Close the dialog box when finished and reset the picture.
18. The **Picture** toolbar contains brightness and contrast controls. With the picture selected, click **More Contrast**, , four times.
19. This is too dark - click **Less Contrast**, , twice.
20. To increase the brightness, click **More Brightness**, , three times.
21. This is too bright; reduce the brightness by clicking **Less Brightness**, , twice.
22. Create a new **Title Only** slide and name it **Transparency**.
23. Insert this **Clip Art** image using the search **animal**:

24. The clip must be converted to a drawing object before it can be made semi transparent. Right click on it and select **Grouping | Ungroup**.
25. Select **Yes** at the prompt.
26. Now right click on the object and select **Format Object**.

Driving Lesson 21 - Continued

27. Select the **Colors and Lines** tab and enter **70** in the **Transparency** box.

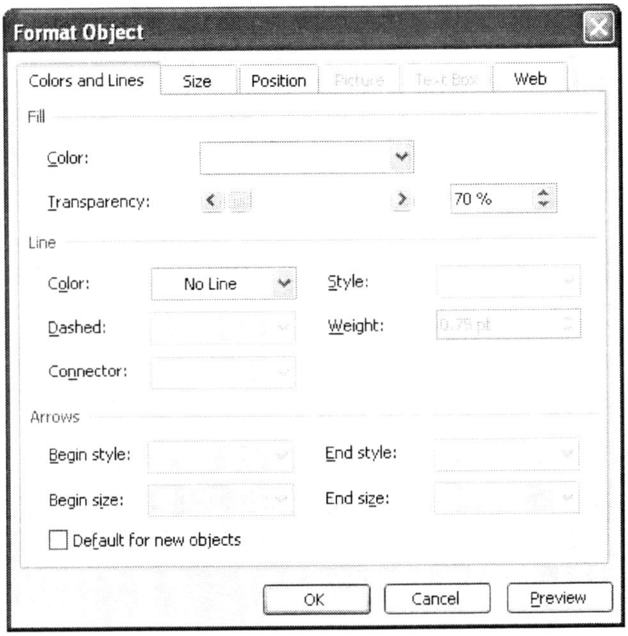

28. Click **OK**. Drag the object over the title and notice how the text can still be seen.

29. Close the presentation <u>without</u> saving.

Driving Lesson 22 - Different Image Formats

Park and Read

Images can be saved in various file formats. Some high quality images such as bitmaps have a larger file size than others. These will take much longer to display and this can be undesirable if the presentation is to be displayed on the Internet - download times will be longer. If an image is saved as a jpg, it will be displayed more quickly, it will make the overall file size smaller and it will still be of a good enough quality to use in your presentation.

Manoeuvres

1. Start a new blank presentation and create a **Blank** slide.
2. Use **Insert | Picture | From File** to insert the **ostrich** image (a **.gif** file) from the supplied data folder.
3. Right click on the image and select **Save as Picture**.
4. Select the supplied data folder as the location for the save.
5. Change the file name to **ostrich2** and select **Device Independent Bitmap** from the **Save as type** drop down list.

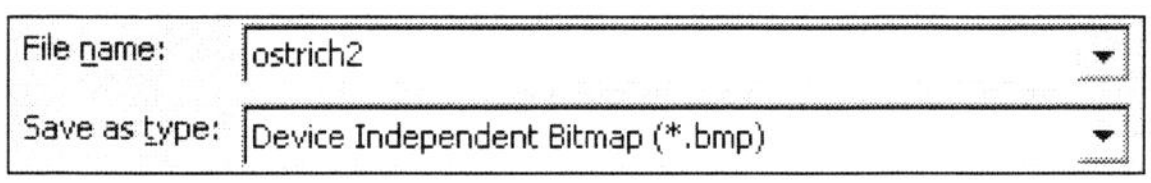

6. Click **Save**. The image is saved in a new format.
7. Select **Save As Picture** again, this time change the file name to **ostrich3** and the **Save as type** to **JPEG File Interchange Format**. Click **Save**.
8. Save the file again in **Portable Network Graphics** (**.png**) format as **ostrich4**.
9. Use **AutoShapes** to draw a circle on the slide and make sure the shape has a **Fill** colour. Right click on it and select **Save as Picture**.
10. Save the object in **GIF Graphics Interchange Format** (**.gif**) format as **shape5**. Close the presentation without saving.
11. From the desktop or **Start** menu, display the contents of the **My Documents** folder, and navigate to the data folder.
12. Select the view to **Details**. Notice the difference in size between the four versions of the ostrich file.

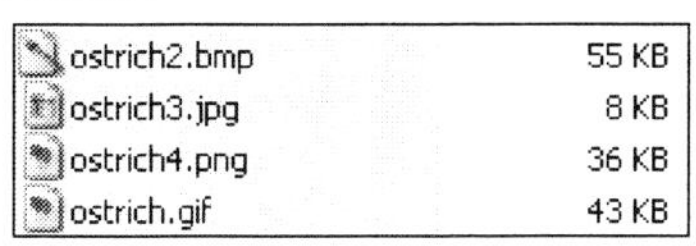

13. Close **Folders View**.

There are many other applications available commercially to manipulate image files, and most of them allow images to be saved in a wide range of formats.

Driving Lesson 23 - Revision

This is not an ECDL test. Testing may only be carried out through certified ECDL test centres. This covers the features introduced in this section. Try not to refer to the preceding Driving Lessons while completing it.

1. Start a new blank presentation with a **Title Only** slide and enter the title **Drawn Objects**.
2. Draw a sun (**AutoShapes | Basic Shapes**), colour it yellow and apply any 3-D style.
3. Draw a square, colour it with a 2 colour **Gradient** effect and make it 3-D.
4. Draw a circle with a **parchment Texture** effect and apply **Shadow Style 12**.
5. Set this effect to be default for all new objects.
6. Draw a circle and an oval.
7. Delete these last two objects.
8. Insert the following **Clip Art** image using the search **nature**.

9. Move or resize the other objects if necessary so that the image fits the slide and no objects overlap.
10. Convert the image to a drawn object.
11. What could you do to the image now that could not be done before it was converted?
12. Change the colour of the roof to red. This will involve several different sections of the image.
13. Save the presentation as **Drawn Objects** and close it.

Check the answers at the back of the guide.

If you experienced any difficulty completing this Revision refer back to the Driving Lessons in this section. Then redo the Revision.

Driving Lesson 24 - Revision

This is not an ECDL test. Testing may only be carried out through certified ECDL test centres. This covers the features introduced in this section. Try not to refer to the preceding Driving Lessons while completing it.

1. Open the **Kittens** presentation.
2. Select the image of the cat on slide **1**.
3. Convert it to **Grayscale**.
4. Now change it to **Washout** style.
5. Move the image over the slide title.
6. Right click the image and select **Order | Send to Back** from the shortcut menu.
7. Close the presentation without saving.
8. Start an image editing application, e.g. *Microsoft Photo Editor* or *Paint*.
9. Open the **cat** image from the data files.
10. Save the file in **JPEG File Interchange Format** with the name **cat edited**.
11. Save the file in **Portable Network Graphics** format with the name **cat saved**.
12. Close the application.

If you experienced any difficulty completing this Revision refer back to the Driving Lessons in this section. Then redo the Revision.

Once you are confident with the features, complete the Record of Achievement Matrix referring to the section at the end of the guide. Only when competent move on to the next Section.

Section 3
Charts

By the end of this Section you should be able to:

Create Combination Charts / 2 Axes Charts

Edit and Format Charts

Create and Edit Flowcharts

Create Cycle and Pyramid Diagrams

Animate Charts

To gain an understanding of the above features, work through the **Driving** Lessons in this **Section**.

For each **Driving Lesson**, read the **Park and Read** instructions, without touching the keyboard, then work through the numbered steps of the **Manoeuvres** on the computer. Complete the **Revision Exercise(s)** at the end of the section to test your knowledge.

Driving Lesson 25 - Combination Charts

Park and Read

A **combination** (or **mixed**) chart shows different types of information by using two or more chart types. For example, a line-column chart may show projected figures as a column chart and actual figures as a line chart on the same grid. A **2 Axes** chart has a different axis on the left and right of the chart so that completely different data can be displayed on the same chart, e.g. rainfall and temperature.

Manoeuvres

1. Start a new blank presentation.
2. Create a new **Title and Chart** slide and add the title **Sales Figures**.
3. Double click where indicated to add the chart. By default a **3D Column** chart is created.
4. To change the chart type select **Chart | Chart Type** and the **Custom Types** tab.
5. Scroll down and select **Line-Column on 2 Axes**.

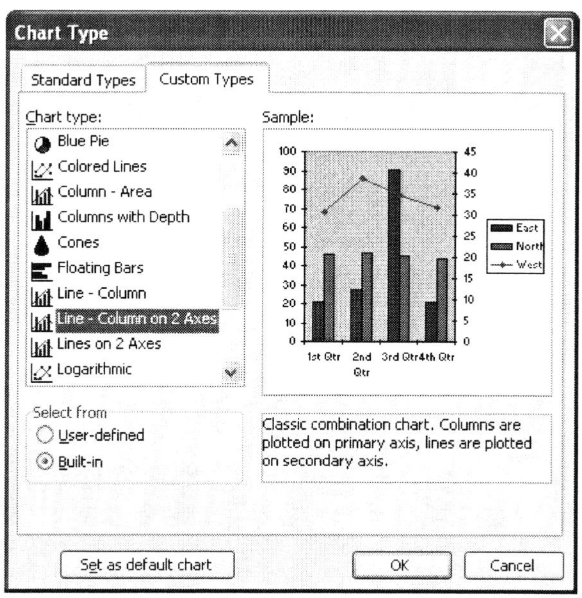

6. Click **OK**.

Driving Lesson 25 - Continued

7. Amend the datasheet as shown below. The units for **Sales Value** (currency) and **Units Sold** (numbers) are different, which is why a 2 axes chart is required.

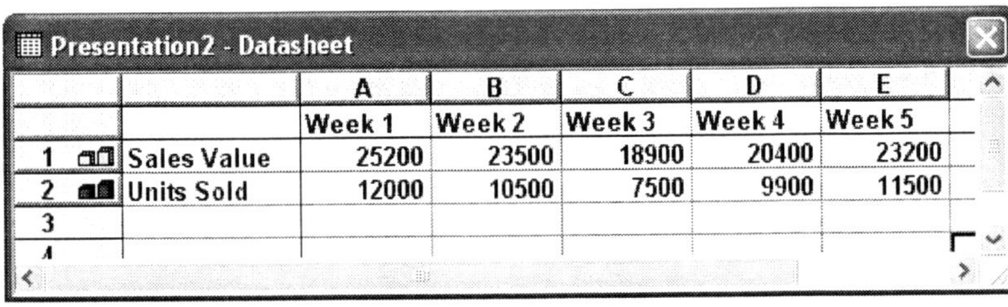
Presentation2 - Datasheet

		A	B	C	D	E
		Week 1	Week 2	Week 3	Week 4	Week 5
1	Sales Value	25200	23500	18900	20400	23200
2	Units Sold	12000	10500	7500	9900	11500
3						
4						

8. Close the datasheet.

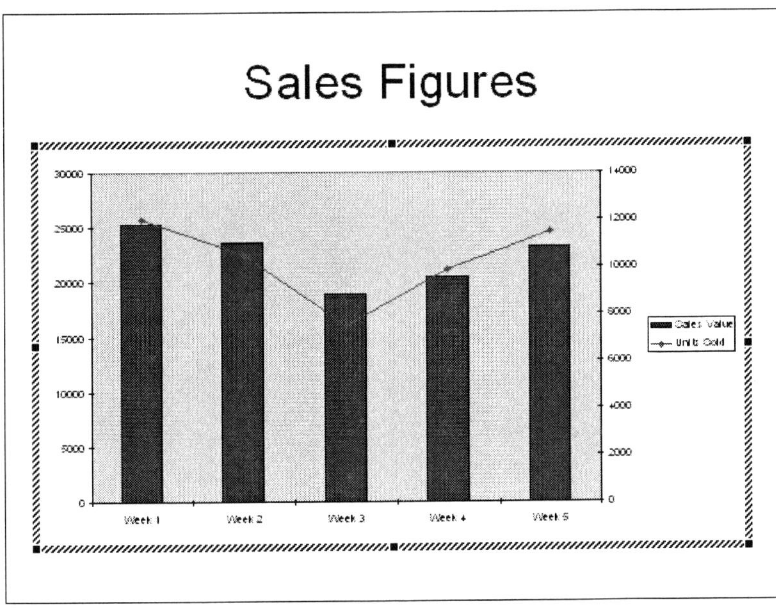

9. The axis for the **Sales Value** figures (blue columns) is on the left and is called the **Value Axis**. The axis for the **Units Sold** figures (red line) is on the right and is called the **Secondary Value Axis**.

10. Save the presentation as **Charts** and leave it open.

Driving Lesson 26 - Editing Charts

Park and Read

Charts can be edited to show data in different ways. The type of the whole chart or a single data series on the chart can be changed; the scale of the value axis and the interval between the plotted numbers can be amended. The way figures are displayed can also be changed. Labels and legends can be formatted.

Manoeuvres

1. With the chart selected, double click on any figure on the **Value Axis** (left) to display the **Format Axis** dialog box and select the **Scale** tab.

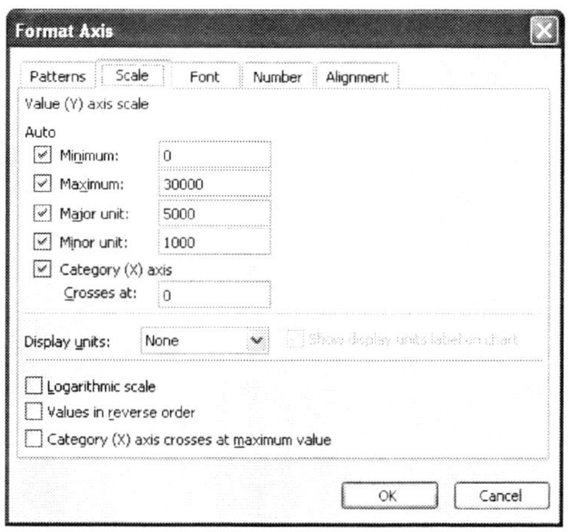

2. No figures below 18900 are shown on the chart, so the lowest figure on the **Value Axis** can be changed to 15000. Change the figure in **Minimum** to **15000**.
3. Change the **Maximum** value to **25000**.
4. The interval between each value on the axis is currently set at **5000**. Change the **Major unit** to **2500**.
5. To change the **Sales Value** units to thousands without amending the datasheet, click the drop down arrow next to **Display units**.
6. Select **Thousands**. There are many different values available - millions and other values can be used. Click **OK**.
7. Notice how the column for **Week 1** is now off the scale of the chart. This is because the **Maximum** value is too low.
8. Change **Maximum** back to **30000**.

Driving Lesson 26 - Continued

9. Double click on any figure on the right axis and amend the **Secondary Value Axis** settings as follows: **Minimum** to **6000**, **Major unit** to **1000** and **Display units** to **Thousands**.

10. Click **OK**.

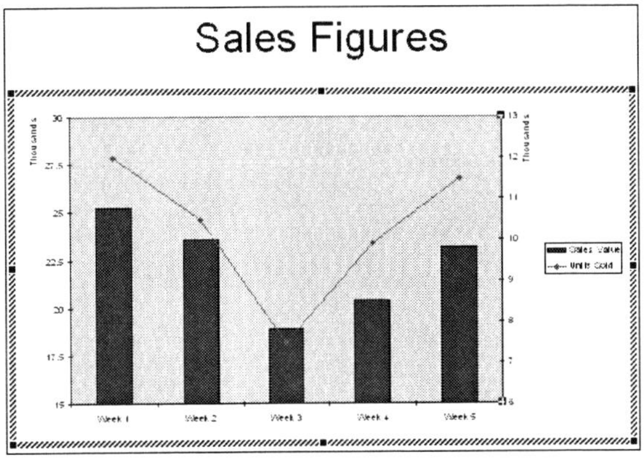

11. Select **Chart | Chart Options** and display the **Titles** tab.

12. Enter a title of **Period 1** and click **OK**.

13. Double click on the title box (not the text) and change the **Area** fill to pale blue. Select the **Font** tab and change the font to **Tahoma**. Click **OK**.

14. Double click on the legend and apply the same fill and font.

15. Select **Chart | Chart Options** and the **Data Labels** tab. Select **Value** to show the actual value on the end of the bars and at each point on the line. Click **OK**.

16. Double click on the data label for any column and select the **Alignment** tab.

17. Select **Inside End** from **Label Position** and from the **Font** tab, change the colour to yellow and click **OK**.

18. Double click on the data label for any line point and select the **Alignment** tab. Select **Above** from **Label Position** and change the **Orientation** to 45^{0}. Click **OK**.

19. Double click on the left **Value Axis** label (**Thousands**) and change the font to **Tahoma**.

20. Repeat this for the right **Secondary Value Axis**, and for the **Category Axis** (**Week 1**, **Week 2,** etc.).

Driving Lesson 26 - Continued

21. Pictures can be applied to various areas on a chart. Double click on the **Chart Area** to display the **Format Chart Area** dialog box, select the **Patterns** tab, **Fill Effects**, **Picture** tab and click **Select Picture**.
22. Browse for the supplied data files and select **Bridge**.
23. Click **Insert**, then click **OK** and **OK** again.
24. Repeat this for the **Plot Area**, this time insert the picture **pink and blue**.
25. Display the **Format Data Series** dialog box for the data columns. Apply the picture **cat** to the columns, selecting **Stack** from the **Picture** tab of the **Fill Effects** dialog box. Click **OK** then **OK** again.

Pictures are applied to bars in bar charts in the same way.

26. This is quite confusing visually. Change it back to a solid blue column.
27. To change the chart type for one data series only, make sure the **Sales Value** data series is selected, then select **Chart | Chart Type** and the **Standard Types** tab.
28. Select **Line** and make sure **Apply to selection** is checked, then click **OK**.
29. The yellow line is difficult to see. Double click on it to display the **Format Data Series** dialog box and change the line colour to dark blue.
30. Change the font colour for the data labels to dark blue.

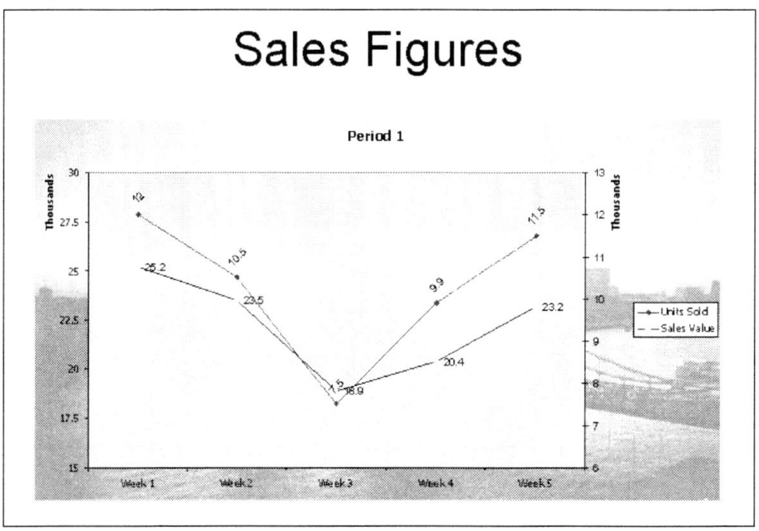

Driving Lesson 26 - Continued

31. To change the entire chart, select **Chart | Chart Type** again with no data series selected. Select the **Column** chart, first subtype, then click **OK**.

32. The new chart type now has only one vertical axis starting at **15** (thousand) and the **Units Sold** data is not seen. Double click on an axis figure to display the **Format Axis** dialog box, and under the **Scale** tab set the **Minimum** value back to **0**. Click **OK**.

33. Right click on any column and select **Format Data Series**. Select the **Options** tab.

34. To change the width of the columns, decrease **Gap width** to **50** using the spinners. The preview will show the columns widening as the gap width is decreased.

35. Change **Overlap** to **- 50**. The columns will separate.

36. Change **Overlap** to **50**. The columns will overlap.

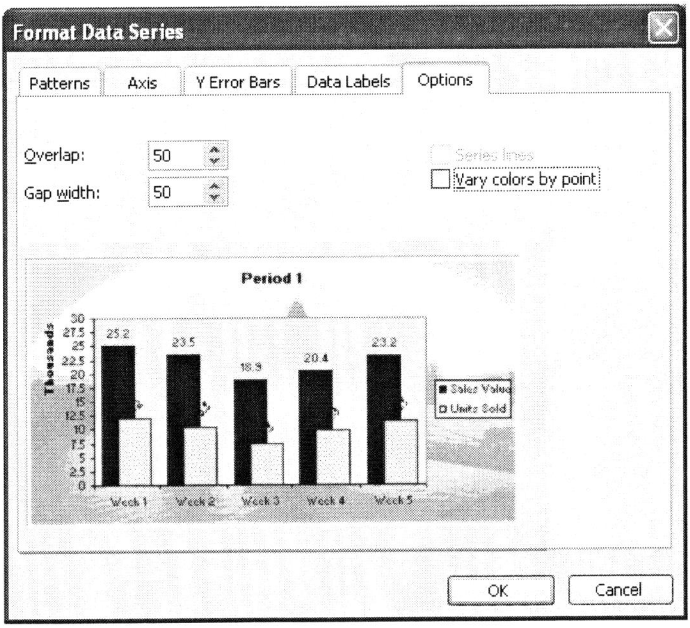

37. Click **OK** to apply the effect to the chart.

38. Save the presentation and leave it open.

Driving Lesson 27 - Animating Charts

Park and Read

Charts can be animated so that the information is displayed gradually in a specified order.

Manoeuvres

1. In the **Charts** presentation, make sure the chart as a whole is selected (with circular handles) but not in edit mode.
2. To animate the chart select **Slide Show | Custom Animation**. From the **Custom Animation Task Pane**, click 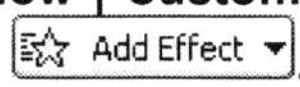
.
3. Select **Entrance** and then **Checkerboard**.
4. Click the drop down arrow at the right of **Chart 2**, 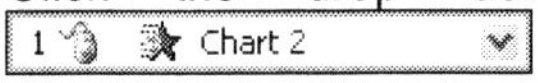

and select **Effect Options**.
5. Select the **Chart Animation** tab. From the **Group chart** drop down list select **By category**. Make sure **Animate grid and legend** is selected.

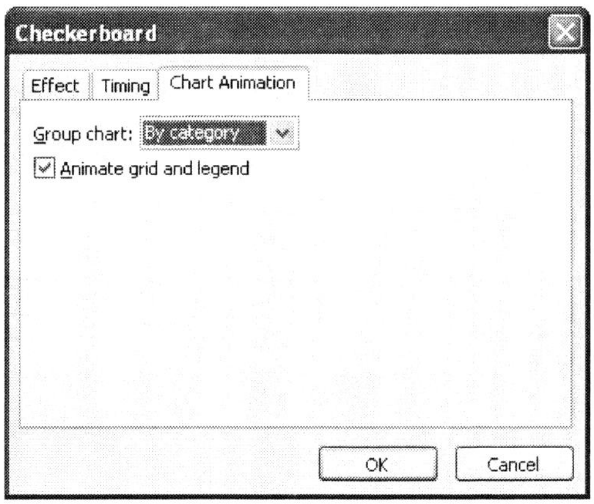

6. Click **OK** then run the slide show. A mouse click is required to display the chart background then each further click displays another category.
7. End the slide show and edit the animation **Effect Options** again. To change the order in which the data is animated, change **Group chart** to **By series**. Uncheck the **Animate grid and legend** option and click **OK**.
8. Run the slide show. Now the background appears automatically and each click displays a complete data series.
9. End the slide show and edit the animation **Effect Options** again. Change **Group chart** to **By element in series**. Check the **Animate grid and legend** option and click **OK**.
10. Run the slide show. Now the background only appears when the mouse is clicked and each further click displays one column in a data series.
11. End the show, save the presentation and leave it open.

Driving Lesson 28 - Creating a Flowchart

Park and Read

Flowcharts on slides can be created by combining preset **AutoShapes** available within *PowerPoint*.

Manoeuvres

1. Insert a new **Title Only** slide and name it **Flowchart**.
2. From the **Drawing** toolbar select **AutoShapes | Flowchart** and the **Flowchart: Terminator** shape, .
3. To start the flowchart click and drag the shape at the top left of the slide and type in **Sales Records**. Flowchart shapes can be moved, resized and coloured like any other drawn object.
4. Beneath this shape draw a **Flowchart: Decision** shape, and type **New Customer?**
5. Complete the flowchart as below, using **Decision**, **Process** and **Terminator** shapes. Press <**Enter**> to start a new line where necessary when typing.

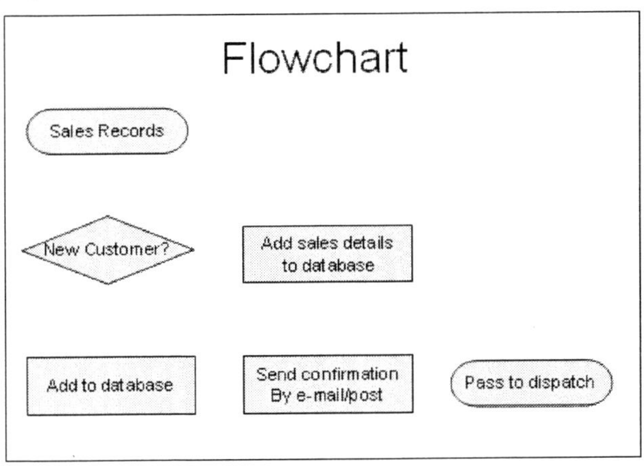

*The **Rectangle** tool can also be used to draw the process shapes and the diamond from **Basic Shapes** to draw the decision shapes.*

Driving Lesson 28 - Continued

6. To connect the shapes select the **Straight Arrow Connector** from **AutoShapes | Connectors** and notice how blue handles appear as the mouse is moved over the shapes.

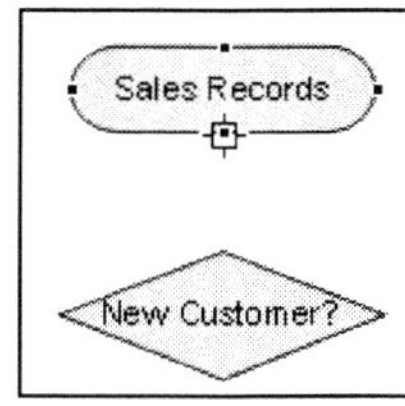

7. Click on the bottom centre handle of the **Sales Records** shape.
8. Move the mouse pointer to the top of the **New Customer?** shape. The line will 'snap' into place when it is close to the correct location. Click once to anchor the line.
9. Select the **Elbow Arrow Connector** and join **New Customer** to **Add sales details to database**.

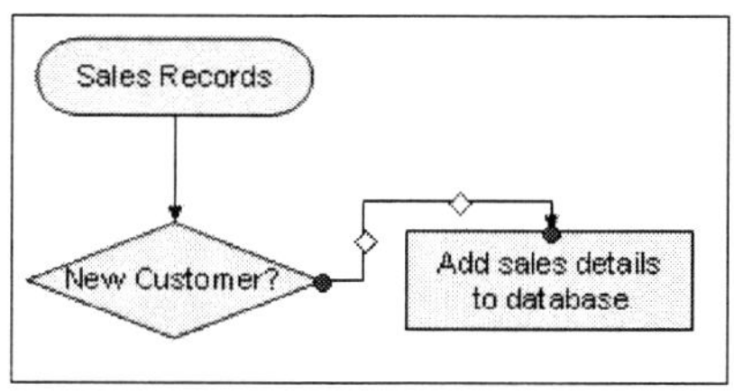

10. Join the other shapes as below and line them up using **Draw | Align or Distribute...**

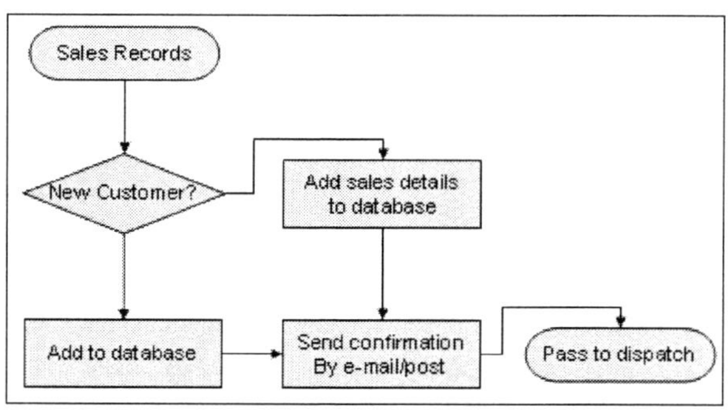

11. Save the presentation and leave it open.

*Flowcharts can also be created using other applications and then used in PowerPoint. A flowchart can be created and saved in Visio for example, and then imported into PowerPoint using **Insert | Object**. This object can then be edited using Visio from within PowerPoint by double clicking on it.*

Driving Lesson 29 - Amending a Flowchart

Park and Read

The shape and position of components used in a flowchart can be changed or deleted as necessary.

Manoeuvres

1. Using the flowchart created in the previous Driving Lesson, add a new terminator shape beneath **Pass to dispatch** and type in **End**.

2. The **Pass to dispatch** shape is the wrong type. Delete it by clicking on the border of the shape and then pressing <**Delete**>.

3. Insert a **Flowchart: Predefined Process** shape, and type in the text **Pass to dispatch**.

4. Connect it to the **End** shape with a **Straight Arrow Connector**.

Connectors can be repositioned by clicking to select them and then dragging any of the marked points.

5. Delete the connector between **Add to database** and **Send confirmation...** by clicking on it and then pressing <**Delete**>.

6. **Add to database** should be linked to **Add sales details....** Select an **Elbow Arrow Connector** and join **Add to database** to the corner of the existing connector from **New Customer?** as shown below:

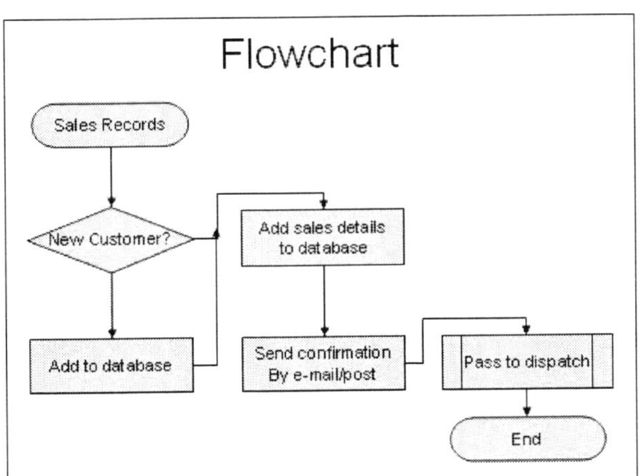

7. Save the presentation and close it.

Driving Lesson 30 - Creating Other Diagrams

Park and Read

PowerPoint helps you create various diagrams to help explain concepts in your presentation. Types available include **cycle diagrams**, which show the circular relationships between related processes, and **pyramid diagrams**, which are divided into horizontal slices to represent a hierarchy.

Manoeuvres

1. Open the presentation **Theatre**.
2. Select slide **5 Workshops** and insert a new slide with a **Title and Diagram or Organization Chart** layout.
3. Add the title **Workshop Teaching Cycle**.
4. Double click the icon to display the **Diagram Gallery** and select the **Cycle Diagram**.

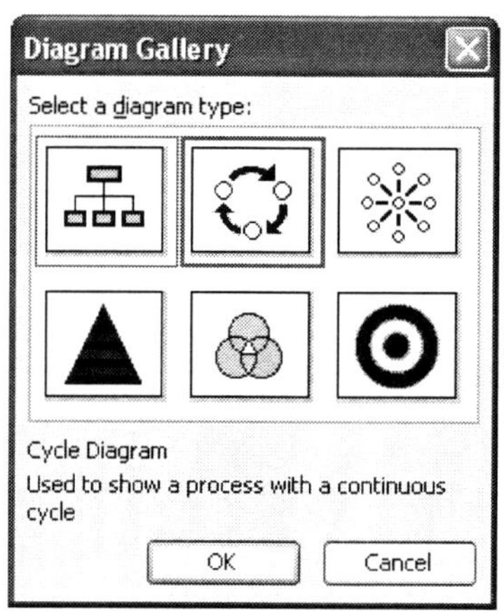

5. Click **OK**.
6. The first area is selected. Click and add the text **Practise and learn**.
7. Click on the bottom area and enter **Test**.
8. Enter **Assess** in the remaining area.

Driving Lesson 30 - Continued

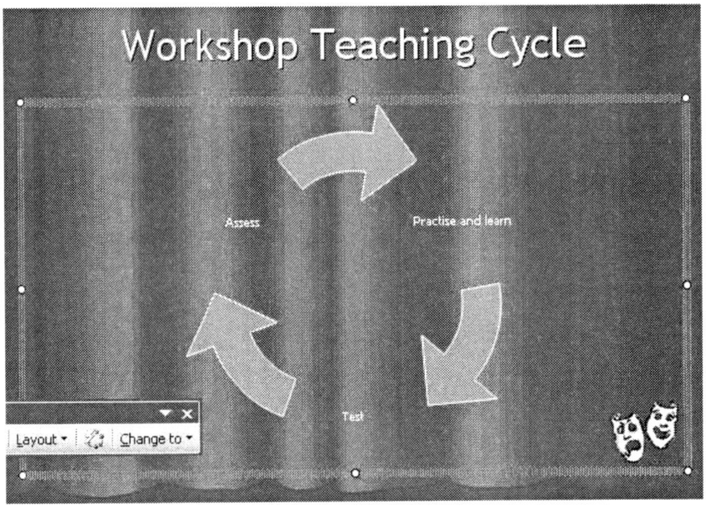

9. Insert a new **Title and Diagram or Organization Chart** slide after slide **2**.
10. This time add the title **Organisation** and insert a **Pyramid Diagram**.
11. On the bottom level enter **Support Staff**, on the middle level enter **Administration**, and on the top level enter **Director**.
12. Click **AutoFormat** on the **Diagram** toolbar, , select **3-D color** then **OK**.
13. Click on the **Director** level and select **Insert Shape** from the **Diagram** toolbar. A new shape is added. Type in **Management**.
14. With this shape selected, click from the **Diagram** toolbar. The shape is moved up the pyramid.
15. To remove it, right click on the shape (not the text) and select **Delete Shape**.
16. Individual shapes can be moved out of a diagram, but only if the **AutoLayout** feature is switched off. Click **Layout** on the **Diagram** toolbar and if **AutoLayout** is selected, click on it to deselect it.
17. Click on the top shape in the pyramid (so that the cursor is a four-way arrow) and drag it to the right. Drag the second shape in the pyramid to the left.
18. Click **Layout** on the **Diagram** toolbar and click **AutoLayout**. The shapes are returned to their original positions.
19. Save the presentation as **Theatre3** and close it.

Driving Lesson 31 - Revision

This is not an ECDL test. Testing may only be carried out through certified ECDL test centres. This covers the features introduced in this section. Try not to refer to the preceding Driving Lessons while completing it.

1. Open the **Assessment** presentation.
2. At the end of the presentation insert a new **Title and Chart** slide.
3. Name it **Pass Rates**.
4. Add a **Line-Column** chart.
5. Amend the datasheet as below.

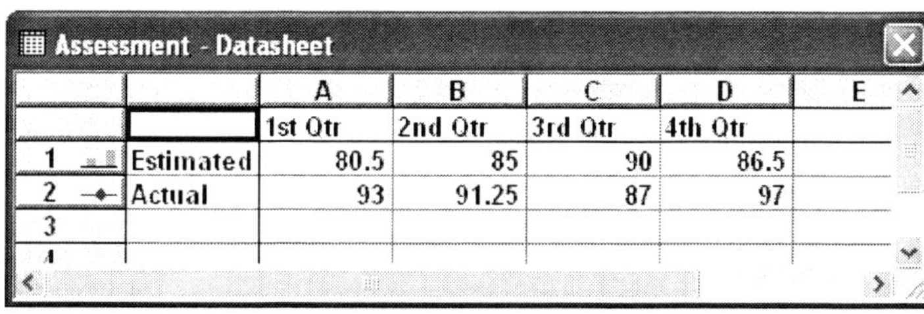

Assessment - Datasheet

		A	B	C	D	E
		1st Qtr	2nd Qtr	3rd Qtr	4th Qtr	
1	Estimated	80.5	85	90	86.5	
2	Actual	93	91.25	87	97	
3						
4						

6. Close the datasheet.
7. Change the **Minimum** scale to **70** and the **Maximum** scale to **100**.
8. Animate the chart to introduce elements **by Category** with the effect **Wipe From Left**.
9. Save the presentation as **Revision31**.
10. View the slide show for this slide and use the mouse button to introduce each section of the chart.
11. Close the presentation.

If you experienced any difficulty completing this Revision refer back to the Driving Lessons in this section. Then redo the Revision.

Driving Lesson 32 - Revision

This is not an ECDL test. Testing may only be carried out through certified ECDL test centres. This covers the features introduced in this section. Try not to refer to the preceding Driving Lessons while completing it.

1. Start a new blank presentation.
2. Create the flowchart shown below on a blank slide. The text is **18pt bold**.

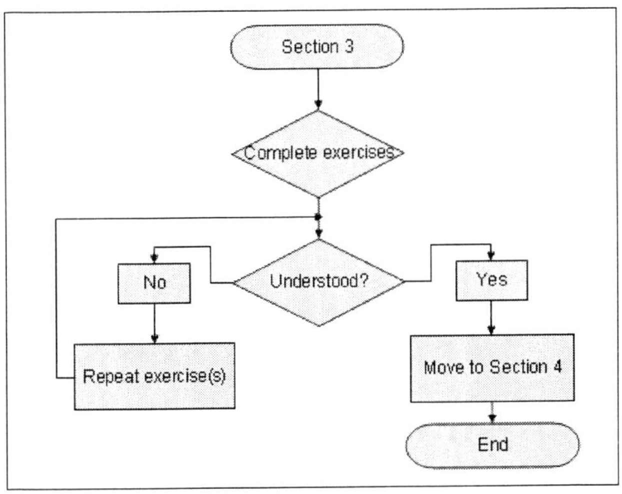

3. The **Complete exercises** shape should be a **Process** shape. Change it.
4. Add a new slide and create a pyramid diagram with 3 levels.
5. The bottom level is **Learn**, then **Practise**, then **Understand**.
6. Format the diagram in any way you like.
7. Save the presentation as **Section 3**.
8. Close it.

If you experienced any difficulty completing this Revision refer back to the Driving Lessons in this section. Then redo the Revision.

Once you are confident with the features, complete the Record of Achievement Matrix referring to the section at the end of the guide. Only when competent move on to the next Section.

Section 4
Multimedia

By the end of this Section you should be able to:

Insert Sounds and Movies

Change Animation Settings

Change Animation Sequence

To gain an understanding of the above features, work through the **Driving Lessons** in this **Section**.

For each **Driving Lesson**, read the **Park and Read** instructions, without touching the keyboard, then work through the numbered steps of the **Manoeuvres** on the computer. Complete the **Revision Exercise(s)** at the end of the section to test your knowledge.

Driving Lesson 33 - Inserting Sounds

Park and Read

A sound can be inserted on to a slide and will then play when that slide is viewed in the slide show. An audio track from a CD can also be inserted.

Manoeuvres

1. Open the presentation **Holiday Choice** and move to slide **2**.
2. To insert a sound select **Insert | Movies and Sounds | Sound from File**.
3. From **Look in** select **Local Disk (C:)/Windows/Media** and select the **chord.wav** file (this is an example of a sound file, if you can't locate it, choose any other).
4. Click **OK** and the following prompt appears.

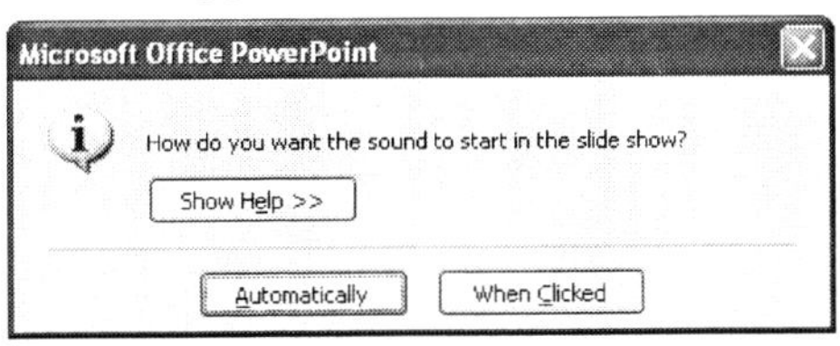

5. Click **Automatically** to play the sound automatically. The sound is added to the slide and is shown as a small icon.
6. Click the **Slide Show** button. The sound will play when the slide appears. Press <**Esc**>.
7. To control when the sound will play, select **Slide Show | Custom Animation**.
8. In the **Task Pane** click the drop down arrow for the sound file (it may be called **Media 6**) and select **Timing**.

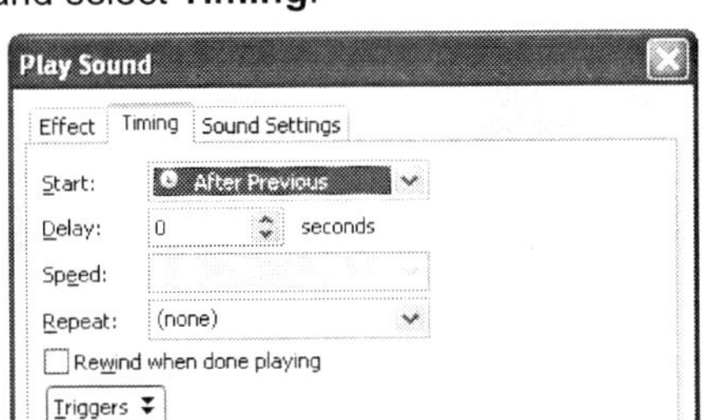

9. To change the timing, set the **Start** to **After Previous** with a **Delay** of 5 seconds.

Driving Lesson 33 - Continued

10. Click **OK** then click the **Slide Show** button. The slide will appear and 5 seconds later the sound will play.
11. Press <**Esc**>.
12. To create a 'previous event' to trigger the sound, select the sandcastle. Click **Add Effect** from the **Task Pane**.
13. Select **Entrance** and then **Fly In**. **Picture frame 3** appears in the animation order area of the **Task Pane**.
14. Click the **Move Up** button, , from **Re-Order** so that it occurs before the sound, **Media 6**. Now the sound will play 5 seconds after that image is animated.
15. With **Picture frame 3** still selected, click the drop down arrow and select **Timing**.
16. From **Start**, select **After previous**, (which is after the slide opening).
17. Change the **Delay** to 4 seconds.

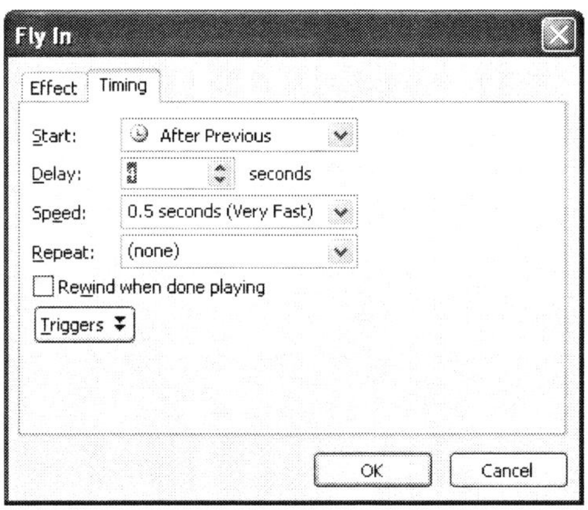

18. Click **OK** to apply the settings.
19. Click the **Slide Show** button, . The slide appears without the sandcastle image. After 4 seconds the image 'zooms' in, and after a further 5 seconds the sound will play.

*To change the effect so that the sound starts on a mouse click, click the drop down arrow for the sound object (**Media**) in the **Custom Animation** task pane, select **Timing**, and from **Start** select **On click**, then click **OK**.*

20. Save the presentation as **Holiday Choice2**.
21. Leave it open for the next Driving Lesson.

Driving Lesson 34 - Inserting Movies

Park and Read

Movies are also easily added to slides.

Manoeuvres

1. Insert a new **Title Only** slide at the end of the presentation.
2. Add the title **Brought to you by:**
3. To insert a video clip select **Insert | Movies and Sounds | Movie from File**.
4. Locate the data folder and select the **cia.avi** file and click **OK**. The following prompt appears:

5. Select **Automatically** so that the movie will automatically play.

6. Click the **Slide Show** button to view the current slide in action.
7. Press <**Esc**> to end the show.
8. To change the movie so that it plays only when the mouse is clicked, select **Slide Show | Custom Animation**.
9. Select the first item in the **Task Pane**.

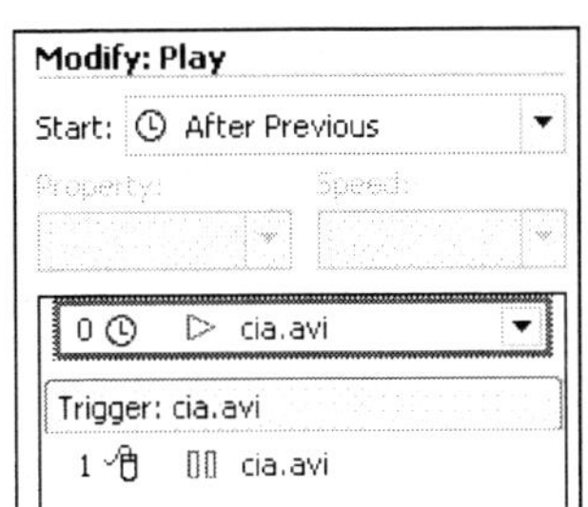

10. Click the **Start** drop down list and select **On Click**.
11. View the slide show for this slide again.
12. Click to see the movie, then press <**Esc**> to end the show.
13. Leave the presentation open for the next Driving Lesson.

Driving Lesson 35 - Introducing Animation

Park and Read

It has been seen that different items on a slide can be animated. These items can be introduced with a click of the mouse, or automatically after a specified time.

Manoeuvres

1. Using the **Holiday Choice2** presentation, move to slide **1**.
2. Make sure the **Custom Animation Task Pane** is displayed.
3. Select the slide title and then click **Add Effect**.
4. Select **Entrance | More Effects** and then **Wedge**. Click **OK**.
5. Make sure **Start** shows **On Click**.
6. Now select the picture and click **Add Effect**.
7. Choose **Entrance | More Effects**, scroll down to the bottom of the dialog box and select **Pinwheel**.

8. Click **OK**.
9. From the **Task Pane**, select the entry for the **Title** and click the drop down arrow.
10. Choose **Effect Options** and from the **Sound** drop down list select **Drum Roll**. Click **OK**.
11. Apply the sound **Laser** to the event **Picture frame 1**.
12. View the slide show. Click to display the text and click again to reveal the picture, then end the show.
13. Apply timing, to start **After previous** with a delay of **4** seconds, to both objects.
14. Click **OK** and view the show again but this time do not click the mouse button. Notice now the animation is activated automatically.
15. End the show, but leave the presentation open.

Driving Lesson 36 - Animation Sequences

Park and Read

The order in which objects are animated can be changed. What happens after they are animated can also be specified.

Manoeuvres

1. View slide **1** of the **Holiday Choice2** presentation in **Normal View**.
2. To apply the picture's animation first, from the **Custom Animation Task Pane**, select **Picture frame 1** and click the **Re-Order Up** button, .

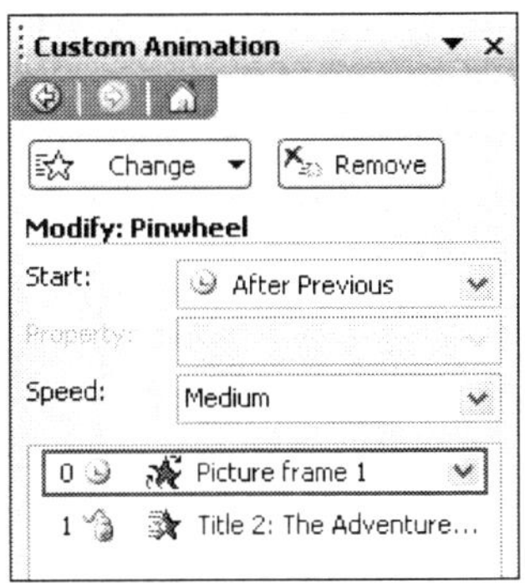

3. View the slide show for the first slide and notice how the picture now appears first.
4. End the show.
5. Change the animation sequence back to how it was originally.
6. Save the changes to the presentation and close it.
7. Open the **Kittens** presentation and move to slide **2**.
8. Use **AutoShapes | Basic Shapes** to draw a small smiley face at the left of the title text and colour it yellow.
9. Select the bulleted list on the left of the slide and in the **Task Pane** apply the **Entrance** effect **Fly In**.
10. Click the drop down arrow on the text object in the **Custom Animation** task pane and select **Effect Options**.
11. From the dialog box, make sure **Direction** is **From Bottom** and **Animate text** is set to **All at once**.

Driving Lesson 36 - Continued

12. To change the appearance of the bulleted points after they have been animated, from **After animation** drop down the list and select a **Red** colour.

After animation *effects can be applied to any text or image.*

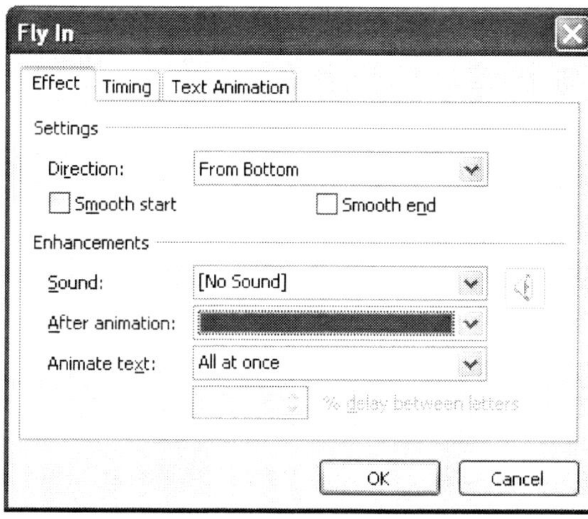

13. Click **OK**.
14. Apply the same animation effects and options to the list on the right.
15. Select the smiley face and apply the **Entrance** effect **Pinwheel**. In **After animation** select **a gray** colour to dim the object.
16. To change the sequence of the animation effects just applied, in the **Task Pane**, move the smiley face up to the top of the list.
17. View the slide show for slide 2 only, clicking the mouse to view the effects. The slide will appear with only the title and the cat image displayed. The first click will introduce the face (yellow). At the next click the face will turn gray, and the first line of text will appear. As the mouse is repeatedly clicked, each item of text will turn red as the next is displayed.
18. End the show and close the presentation <u>without</u> saving.

To remove a custom animation effect, click on the drop down arrow for the effect in the ***Custom Animation*** *task pane and select* ***Remove****.*

Driving Lesson 37 - Revision

This is not an ECDL test. Testing may only be carried out through certified ECDL test centres. This covers the features introduced in this section. Try not to refer to the preceding Driving Lessons while completing it.

1. Open the presentation **Assessment**.
2. View slide **4** in **Normal View**.
3. View the **Custom Animation Task Pane**.
4. Change the animation order for **Shape 11 Open** to appear immediately after **Text 2** (position **3**).
5. Apply a different **Entrance** animation effect to each of the puzzle pieces (**Shape 3** to **Shape 11**).
6. View the slide show for this slide. Do not click the mouse button. All elements of the slide will eventually appear in turn.
7. Close the presentation without saving.

If you experienced any difficulty completing this Revision refer back to the Driving Lessons in this section. Then redo the Revision.

Driving Lesson 38 - Revision

This is not an ECDL test. Testing may only be carried out through certified ECDL test centres. This covers the features introduced in this section. Try not to refer to the preceding Driving Lessons while completing it.

1. Open the presentation **Kittens**.
2. On slide **1** apply an **Entrance** animation effect of **Zoom** to the picture of the cat (**Picture frame 3**). The effect is to be started by a mouse click.
3. Insert the **Growl** sound from the supplied data files as a separate item.
4. Set the sound up to play **automatically**, **4** seconds after the previous event (that is 4 seconds after the cat image appears).
5. View the slide show for slide **1** to hear the sound.
6. Close the presentation <u>without</u> saving.

If you experienced any difficulty completing this Revision refer back to the Driving Lessons in this section. Then redo the Revision.

Once you are confident with the features, complete the Record of Achievement Matrix referring to the section at the end of the guide. Only when competent move on to the next Section.

Section 5
Slide Shows

By the end of this Section you should be able to:

Create and Edit Action Buttons/Hyperlinks

Create and Edit Custom Shows

Run a Custom Show

Apply Slide Transitions

Apply Timings

Set up a Slide Show

Use Various Techniques while Running a Show

To gain an understanding of the above features, work through the **Driving Lessons** in this **Section**.

For each **Driving Lesson**, read the **Park and Read** instructions, without touching the keyboard, then work through the numbered steps of the **Manoeuvres** on the computer. Complete the **Revision Exercise(s)** at the end of the section to test your knowledge.

Driving Lesson 39 - Action Buttons

Park and Read

Action buttons can be added to allow rapid and easy navigation between slides during the presentation using **hyperlinks**. Action buttons also allow movement to other presentations, files, web sites and various other destinations.

Manoeuvres

1. Open the **Assessment2** presentation and save it as **Assessment3**.
2. Close the **Task Pane** and move to slide **4**, title **The Open Learning Guide**.
3. To create an action button that links to slide **7**, click the **AutoShapes** button, AutoShapes, then **Action Buttons** and finally select the **Information** action button, .
4. Click and drag the shape of the button on the bottom left side of the slide.

*If a message appears about saving the presentation, select **Yes**.*

5. The **Action Settings** dialog box appears. Ensure that the **Mouse Click** tab is selected. Click the **Hyperlink to** option and from the drop down list, select **Slide**. From the list of slides displayed, select slide **7 Where to Get More Information**. Click **OK**.

Driving Lesson 39 - Continued

6. Click **OK** again.

*To remove a hyperlink, display the **Action Settings** dialog box for the object containing the link and select **None** from **Action on click**.*

7. Click the **Slide Show** button to see the slide as it will appear in the presentation.
8. When the cursor appears, click the action button. The presentation moves to the **Where to Get More Information** slide.
9. The presentation will continue from its new position (there is no automatic return to the original slide). Click until the show is ended.
10. With slide **7** displayed in **Normal View**, draw a **Custom** action button, ☐, at the bottom left of the slide, which will link to a separate presentation.
11. In the **Action Settings** dialog box, select **Hyperlink to** and then **Other PowerPoint Presentation**.
12. Select **CIA Seminar** from the list.

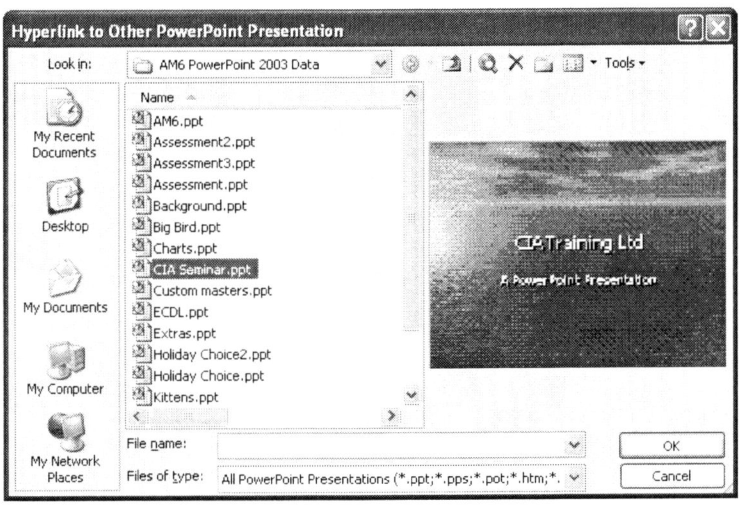

13. Click **OK** and ensure **Hyperlink To Slide** shows **Slide 1** highlighted and then click **OK**.
14. Click **OK** to insert the button and with the button selected type **CIA** so it is labelled.
15. View the slide show and test the button. Click to view the **CIA Seminar** show. End that show to return to the **Assessment3** show.

Driving Lesson 39 - Continued

16. Press <**Esc**> to end that show and return to **Normal View**.
17. At the bottom left of slide **5** draw a **Document** action button, . This will link to a *Word* document.
18. From **Action Settings** select **Hyperlink to | Other File**.
19. Choose the **Sample** file and click **OK** then **OK** again.
20. Run the show and after the text has loaded click the action button. *Word* starts and opens the document.
21. Close *Word*, without saving if prompted and end the show.
22. Move to slide **7**. There is already a text hyperlink to the **CiA** website, but an action button can also be created.

*Dynamic links can also be applied to text or graphical objects - you don't always have to use action buttons. Select the text or object, right click on it and select **Action Settings** from the shortcut menu. This displays the same dialog box as appears when you draw an action button. Alternatively, select the item, then **Insert | Hyperlink**. Choose where to link to from the left of the dialog box and click **OK**.*

23. Draw a custom action button at the right of the existing one.
24. From **Hyperlink to** select **URL**.
25. Type in the following address:

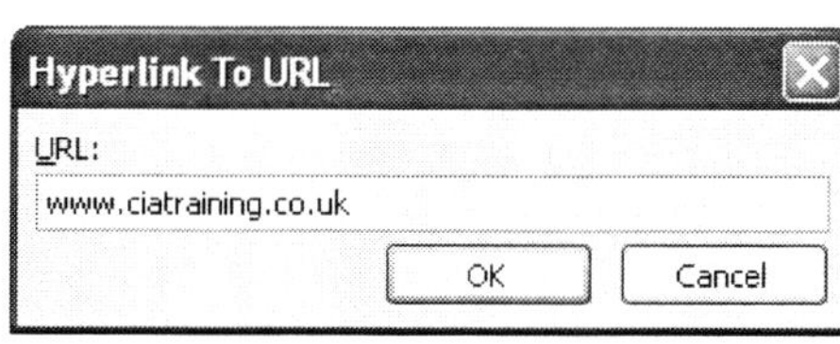

26. Click **OK** and **OK** again.
27. With the button selected, type in **Web Site** to be the button label.
28. Resize the button to fit the text.
29. Run the show and click the action button. Your browser application will start and if an Internet connection exists, the CiA Training home page will be displayed.
30. Close the browser and end the show.
31. Save the presentation and close it.

Driving Lesson 40 - Editing an Action Button

Park and Read

It is possible to change the destination of an action button after creating it. This may be necessary if a web address (**URL**) or a file location changes.

Manoeuvres

1. Open the **Assessment3** presentation. On slide **7** right click on the **CiA** action button, (but not on the text content), at the far left of the screen.
2. Select **Edit Hyperlink**. The current hyperlink destination is shown.

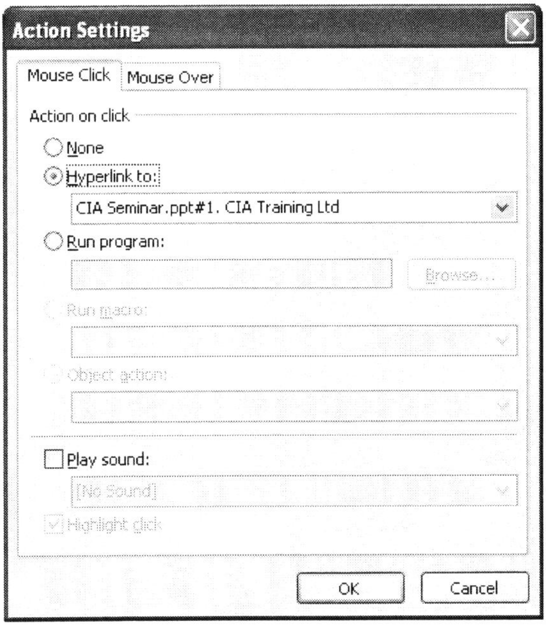

3. To change the link to a different presentation, click the drop down list and select **Other PowerPoint Presentation**.
4. Select the **Holiday Choice** presentation from the data files and click **OK**, then **OK** again to hyperlink to the first slide.
5. Click **OK** in the **Action Settings** dialog box.
6. View the slide show for this slide and when the text has loaded click the button to view the linked presentation.

Driving Lesson 40 - Continued

7. End both shows.
8. Right click on the **CiA Web** button and select **Edit Hyperlink**.
9. Drop down the list and select **URL**.
10. To link to a different web page change the address in **Hyperlink to URL** to **www.ecdl.com** and click **OK**, then **OK** again.
11. Change the text on the button to **Ecdl** by clicking and dragging to select the existing text and overtyping.

*Any action button can have its destination changed in this way, whether it's to a slide, a presentation, a file, URL, etc. Remember, to remove the hyperlink, select **None** from **Action on click** in the **Action Settings** dialog box. To remove a hyperlink that has been created via the **Insert Hyperlink** dialog box, right click on the item containing the link and select **Remove Hyperlink**.*

12. If you have an Internet connection, run the show and click the button when the text has loaded.
13. View the site.
14. Close the browser and end the show.
15. Close the presentation <u>without</u> saving.

Driving Lesson 41 - Custom Shows

Park and Read

Custom shows allow different parts of one presentation to be shown as different shows to different audiences without the need for creating multiple versions of the same presentation. For example, an audience of salespeople could see a presentation without seeing those slides relating to administration and training, and finance staff could be given the same presentation, but without the sales and training slides. A custom show can be set up so that certain slides can be missed out when necessary.

Manoeuvres

1. Select **File | New** and from the **Templates** section of the **New Presentation Task Pane**, click **On my computer**. Select the **Presentations** tab, select **Business Plan** and click **OK**.

2. Make sure the left hand pane displays **Slides** then enter either your company name or your own name where indicated on slide **1**. Save the presentation as **Custom**.

3. Select **View | Header and Footer**, check the box to include **Slide number** and click **Apply to All**.

4. The presentation is to be shown to two departments of the same company: **Finance** and **Marketing**. To avoid the creation of two separate presentations, two custom shows are to be created, each showing slightly different slides.

5. Select **Slide Show | Custom Shows** to display the **Custom Shows** dialog box, then click the **New** button to open the **Define Custom Show** dialog box.

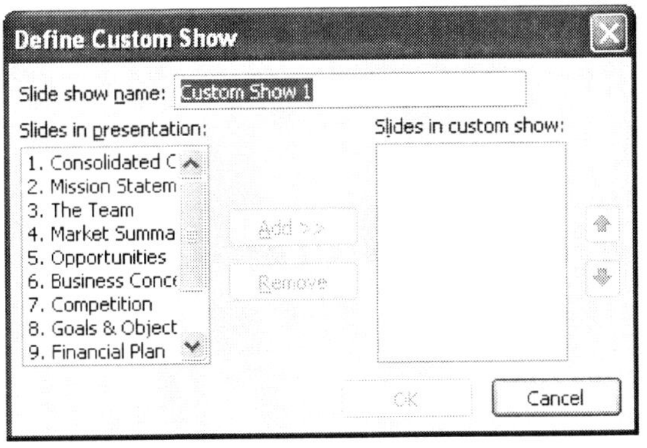

Driving Lesson 41 - Continued

6. Name the custom show **Finance** as this is the show to be given to that department.

7. The **Finance** people do not need to see all of the **Marketing** slides. Select the first slide, then click **Add**.

8. Select slide **2** and then hold down <**Ctrl**> as you select slides **4**, **9**, **11** and **12**. Click **Add** to add them to the custom show, then click **OK** to return to the **Custom Shows** dialog box.

9. Create another custom show called **Marketing** (**Add** slides **1**, **2**, **3**, **4**, **6**, **7** and **12**). Click **OK**.

10. To edit the **Marketing** department's show, select **Marketing** from the list in the **Custom Shows** dialog box.

11. Click **Edit**. Slide **5** is to be removed.

12. Click on slide **5 Business Concept** at the right of the dialog box.

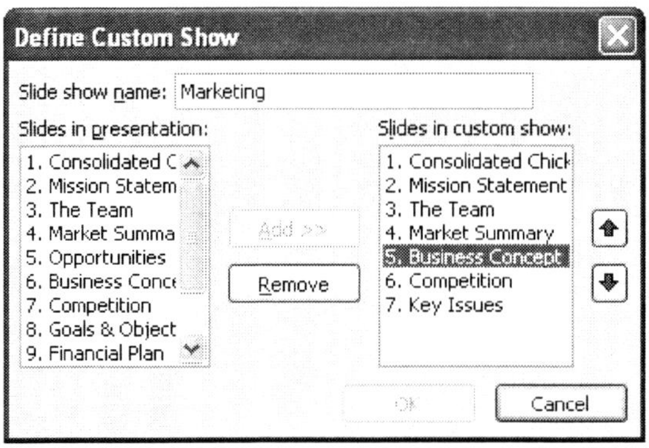

13. Click **Remove**.

14. Slide **4 Market Summary** is to be moved after **Competition**. Select slide **4** from the right of the dialog box.

15. Click **Move Down**, .

16. Click **OK** and then **Close**.

17. Save the presentation and leave it open.

Driving Lesson 42 - Running a Custom Show

Park and Read

After custom shows have been created they can be run via the menus, or more professionally by adding action buttons to the presentation.

Manoeuvres

1. View slide **1** of the **Custom** presentation in **Normal View** and select **Slide Show | Custom Shows**.

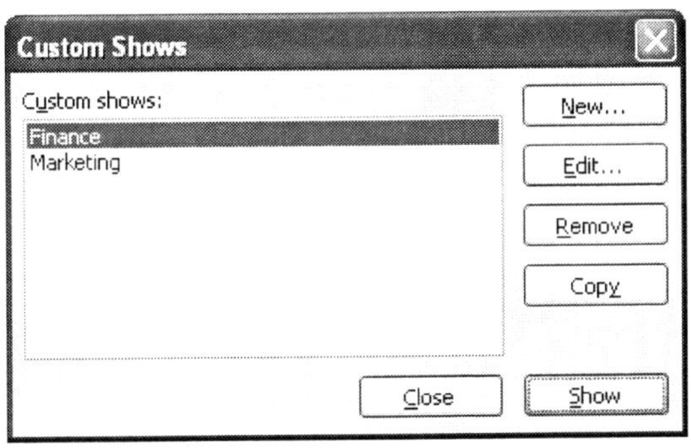

2. To run the **Finance** show, select it from the list and click **Show**.
3. Click the mouse to advance the slides, noting which slides are displayed, and click to exit.
4. View the **Marketing** show in the same way.
5. To create a copy of the **Marketing** show, select it from the **Custom Shows** dialog box and click **Copy**. The new show **Copy of Marketing** appears below the others.
6. A copy is not actually needed. Select **Copy of Marketing** and click **Remove**. Close the **Custom Shows** dialog box.
7. It would be better to select the required show by using action buttons on the first slide. Draw an **Action Button:Custom** at the lower left of slide **1**.
8. Select **Hyperlink to** and from the list select **Custom Show | Finance** then click **OK** and **OK** again.
9. With the button selected type in **Finance**. Click away from the button.
10. Repeat the above steps to create a button for the **Marketing** custom show at the right of the first button.

Driving Lesson 42 - Continued

11. Resize and move the buttons as necessary and change their fill colour to pale green to match the design.
12. Because slide **1** will now always be displayed in order to start the custom shows, you may want to remove it from each show sequence. To remove slide **1**, select **Slide Show | Custom Shows**, select the **Finance** show and click the **Edit** button.
13. Select slide **1** from the list on the right and click **Remove**. Click **OK**. Repeat these steps for the **Marketing** show and close the dialog box.
14. Run the full slide show (12 slides) and then start the show and use the **Finance** button to see that custom show, advancing by clicking. This is easier than using the menus. Notice the slide numbers on all slides.
15. Save the presentation and leave it open.

Driving Lesson 43 - Applying Transitions

Park and Read

To add interest to a slide show, a transition can be applied to slides. This is a special effect, which controls how one slide changes to the next. Timings can be applied to the effects, so that they appear after a specified interval, or they can be displayed manually by clicking the mouse.

Manoeuvres

1. In **Slide Sorter View**, select slide **1**.

2. To create a transition effect, click the **Slide Transition** button, 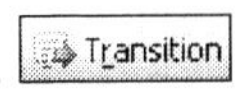

(or select **Slide Show | Slide Transition**). The **Slide Transition Task Pane** appears.

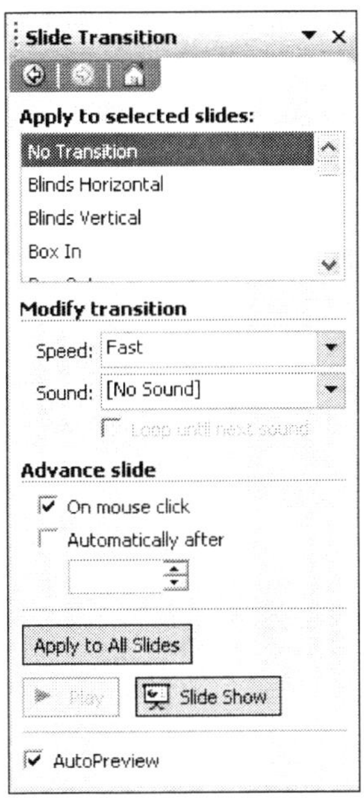

3. Select any effect from the list of transition effects shown. A demonstration of the effect is shown.

4. Try using some of the other effects to see what they do, then scroll down and select **Dissolve**.

5. From **Modify transition** select the speed **Medium** and from **Advance slide** select **On mouse click**, then click **Apply to All Slides**. All slides now have the **Dissolve** transition effect applied.

Driving Lesson 43 - Continued

*Each slide can have a different effect if desired, although normally they would all be the same. To apply an individual effect, select the slide, choose an effect from the **Slide Transition Task Pane** but do not click **Apply to All Slides**.*

6. Select the first slide, then view the slide show. Click the mouse button to move through all the slides and notice the effects as the slides change.

*A slide that has a transition applied has a symbol underneath it in **Slide Sorter** view.*

7. To apply timings to the transition effects select slide **1**.

8. At the moment the effects do not appear until the mouse is clicked. In the **Task Pane**, click in **On mouse click** to remove the check, then check **Automatically after**.

9. Use the up spinner to increase the time to **5** seconds:

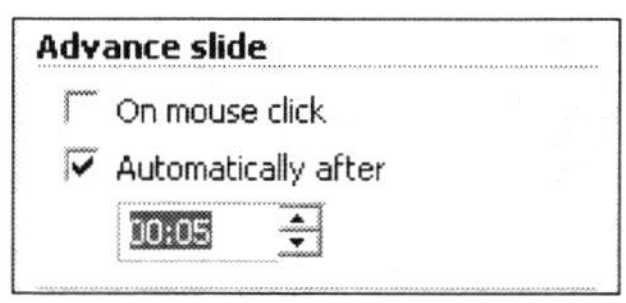

*To remove the transition timing, remove the check from **Automatically after**.*

10. Click **Apply to All Slides**. The transition timing for each slide is now shown underneath the slide image in **Slide Sorter View**.

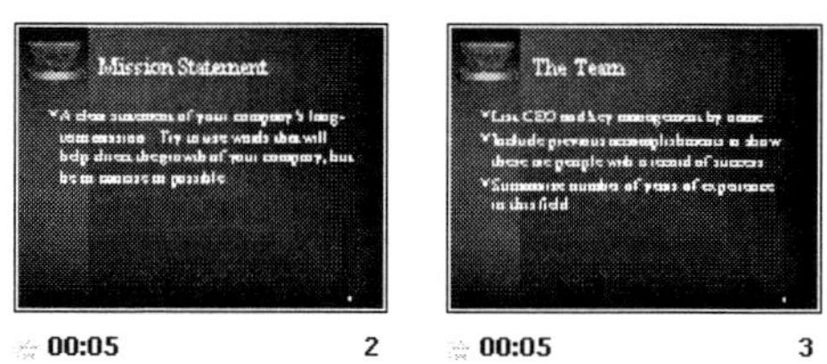

11. View the slide show. Using this option the slide show could be left to run without the need for a presenter, as a continuously running display for example.

12. When the show ends, change the settings back so the transitions are activated when the mouse is clicked.

*It is possible to select both **Advance** options (mouse click and automatic) at the same time. Then each transition can be activated by using the mouse if required, but if this is not used within the set time, the transition will start automatically.*

13. Save the presentation and leave it open for the next exercise.

Driving Lesson 44 - Applying Timings

Park and Read

Instead of applying timings to slide transitions, slide shows can also have timings applied to each slide separately. This means that enough time can be allowed to describe each particular slide. These timings are set up during a **Rehearsal**.

If a presentation contains hyperlinks and action buttons it should be run manually, so that the links can be used.

Manoeuvres

1. In **Slide Sorter View**, select the first slide and to apply timings click the **Rehearse Timings** button, (or select **Slide Show | Rehearse Timings**). The slide show begins, with the **Rehearsal** dialog box on the screen.

2. Allow enough time to talk about the slide then click the **Next** button, . The next screen appears with the time for the current slide reset to zero.
3. Pause the rehearsal by clicking , then restart it using the same button. Move to the next slide/effect.
4. View the entire presentation, clicking the **Next** button after the required time period for each slide until finished.
5. At the end of the rehearsal a dialog box appears showing the total time for the slide show and asking if the timings are to be saved for future use.

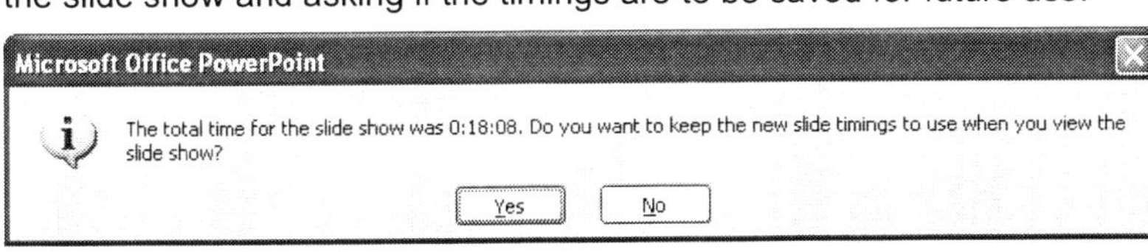

6. Click **Yes**. The individual times for each slide are now displayed. The total time for the slide show is made up of these times. The timings can be changed at any time by clicking the **Rehearse Timings** button again.
7. Individual timings can still be amended. Click on slide **3** and in the **Slide Transition Task Pane**, increase the time value by 5 seconds.
8. Save the presentation and leave it open.

Driving Lesson 45 - Setting up a Slide Show

Park and Read

A slide show can be set up to run in a few different ways. It can be run manually, by clicking the mouse, or automatically using timings. It can also be set up to loop, running continuously. Note that even when timings have been applied to a show, you should check to make sure that it has been set up to use these timings.

Manoeuvres

1. To make sure the timings specified earlier are to be used when the show runs, select **Slide Show | Set Up Show**.
2. In the **Set Up Show** dialog box under **Advance slides**, select the option **Using timings, if present**.

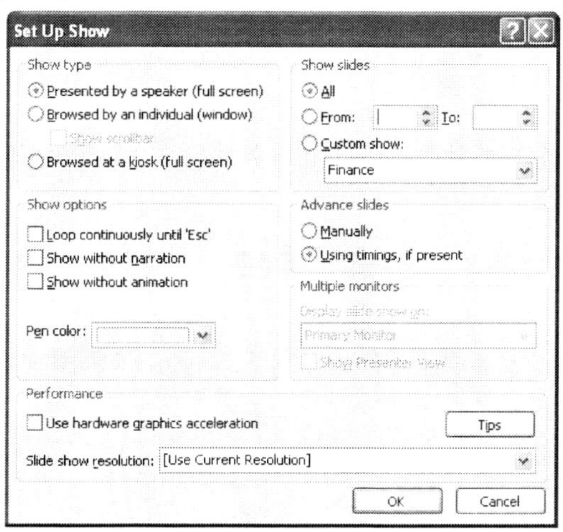

3. Click **OK**, then save the presentation. View the slide show, which will now play using the timings set in the rehearsal. There is no need to click the mouse.
4. In **Slide Sorter View**, select **Slide Show | Set Up Show**.
5. To disable the timings select **Manually** from **Advance slides**. Click **OK**.
6. Check **On mouse click** in the **Task Pane** and click **Apply to All Slides**.
7. Click on the first slide and then view the show.
8. The first slide in the presentation appears. Click the mouse to move to the second slide.

Driving Lesson 45 - Continued

9. Move through the rest of the slide show.

10. At the end of the show *PowerPoint* returns to **Slide Sorter View**. Change the set up within the **Set Up Show** dialog box to use timings again, but don't click **OK** yet (the show could still be advanced using the mouse if desired).

11. To make the show run continuously, check **Loop continuously until 'Esc'**.

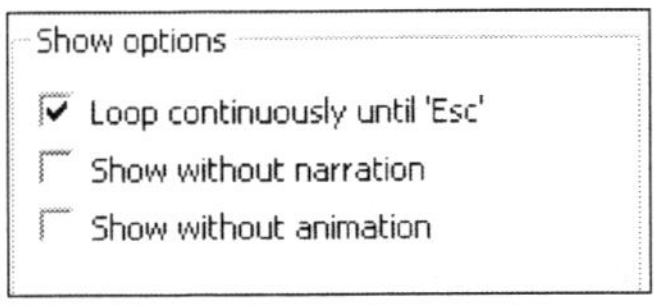

12. Click **OK**.

13. View the show and when the end is reached, the show will start again.

14. Press <**Esc**> to end the slide show.

15. To stop the show looping, select **Slide Show | Set Up Show** and uncheck **Loop continuously....**

16. Click **OK**.

17. Save and close the presentation.

18. Open the presentation **Holiday Choice**.

19. Apply custom animation, an **Entrance** effect of **Fly In**, to the picture on slide **1**.

20. Set **Direction** to **From Left** and use the **Timing** option so that it starts after the previous event with a delay of 3 seconds.

21. View the show for this slide only.

22. The show can also be run without animation. Select **Slide Show | Set Up Show**.

23. Under **Show options**, check **Show without animation** and click **OK**.

24. View the show for this slide again and notice how the picture is not animated.

25. Close the presentation without saving.

Driving Lesson 46 - Slide Show Techniques

Park and Read

While running a show, you may need to pause to expand on a particular point, or indicate areas on a slide. There are various ways of controlling the show and being able to do just that.

Manoeuvres

1. Open the presentation **Theatre**. Select **Slide Show | View Show** to start the slide show. Click on the first slide to move to slide **2**.
2. Right click anywhere on the screen. From the shortcut menu, select **Pointer Options | Felt Tip Pen**. You are going to annotate the slide.
3. Hold down <**Shift**> and draw a line beneath **newly refurbished**. this method could be used to emphasise a point as the show is presented.
4. To remove all pen marks, right click again and select **Pointer Options | Erase All Ink on Slide**.
5. Right click and select **Pointer Options | Arrow**.
6. Right click once more and select **Go to Slide**, then select slide **4**.
7. At this point, you may wish to pause for questions. So there are no distractions, right click and select **Screen | Black Screen**.
8. Click to redisplay the slide, then right click and select **Screen | White Screen**. Click again to resume the show.
9. To end the show at any time, either press <**Esc**> or right click and select **End Show**.
10. Apply a transition effect of your choice to all slides, with automatic timing of **5** seconds.
11. When timings are applied the show can be stopped during its progress. Start the slide show and let it continue to slide **3**.
12. Right click and select **Screen | Pause** to pause the show.
13. Right click again and select **Screen | Resume**.
14. Let the show continue to the end and then click to exit.
15. Close the presentation without saving.

The options on the shortcut menu are also available from the popup buttons in the lower left of the slide show 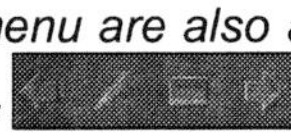.

Driving Lesson 47 - Revision

This is not an ECDL test. Testing may only be carried out through certified ECDL test centres. This covers the features introduced in this section. Try not to refer to the preceding Driving Lessons while completing it.

1. Open the **Kittens** presentation.
2. Create a custom show called **Information** consisting of slides **3**, **4**, **5** and **8**.
3. Create a second custom show called **Charity** consisting of slides **2**, **6** and **7**.
4. Create an action button for each custom show on slide **1**, one at the bottom left of the slide and one at the bottom right.
5. View the slide show from slide **1** and use the action buttons to view each custom show in turn.
6. Use the **Ballpoint Pen** option to draw on slide **2** in the **Charity** custom show - underline **How to make a donation**.
7. Change back to the **Arrow** pointer option.
8. Pause the show by displaying a black screen, the restart it.
9. End the slide show. Select **Discard** when prompted **Do you want to keep your ink annotations**.
10. Save the presentation as **Shelter** and close it.

If you experienced any difficulty completing this Revision refer back to the Driving Lessons in this section. Then redo the Revision.

Driving Lesson 48 - Revision

This is not an ECDL test. Testing may only be carried out through certified ECDL test centres. This covers the features introduced in this section. Try not to refer to the preceding Driving Lessons while completing it.

1. Open the presentation **CIA Seminar**.
2. Apply a **Cover Down** slide transition to all slides.
3. All transitions should be advanced **automatically** after **5** seconds, but also leave the **On mouse click** option selected.
4. Set the speed to **Slow**.
5. Set up the show to use timings and to loop continuously.
6. View the slide show. Use the mouse button on a few slides to override the timings and display a black screen while viewing slide **3**.
7. Continue the show.
8. After it starts for the second time press <**Esc**>.
9. Remove the option to loop continuously.
10. Rehearse timings for the show, advancing slide **1** after about **10** seconds and all others after about **15** seconds.
11. Save the timings.
12. Save the presentation as **Seminar Complete**.
13. View the slide show again.
14. Close the presentation.

If you experienced any difficulty completing this Revision refer back to the Driving Lessons in this section. Then redo the Revision.

Once you are confident with the features, complete the Record of Achievement Matrix referring to the section at the end of the guide.

Section 6
Linking

By the end of this Section you should be able to:

Create a Link to a Text File

Link to a Chart and a Worksheet Range

Link an Image to a File

Modify Linked Data

Break Links and Embed Objects

Edit Embedded Data

Save a Slide as an Image

To gain an understanding of the above features, work through the **Driving Lessons** in this **Section**.

For each **Driving Lesson**, read the **Park and Read** instructions, without touching the keyboard, then work through the numbered steps of the **Manoeuvres** on the computer. Complete the **Revision Exercise(s)** at the end of the section to test your knowledge.

Driving Lesson 49 - Embedding

Park and Read

Objects can be embedded on a slide. This means that a copy of the data is actually stored with the slide and can be edited from the slide. If the source data changes, or is deleted, the data on the slide will be unaffected.

Manoeuvres

1. Open the **Kittens** presentation and save it as **Links**.
2. At the end of the presentation create a new **Title Only** slide and add the title **Embedded Text**.
3. To insert the data, select **Insert | Object** and the **Create from file** option.

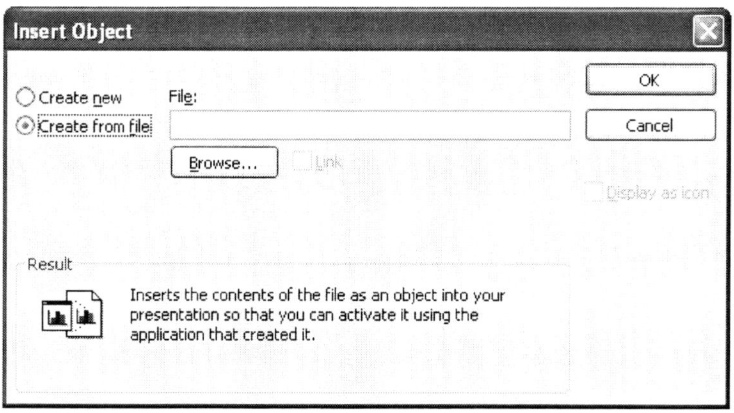

4. Click **Browse** and locate the supplied data files. Select the **Labradors** file and click **OK**.
5. Click **OK** to embed object and then save the presentation.
6. To edit the document, double click the text on the slide. The embedded text is opened in editing view. Select the heading **Our Sanctuary** and underline it.
7. Click on a blank area of the slide to close the editing view.
8. Leave the presentation open.

Driving Lesson 50 - Linking Text

Park and Read

Objects on a slide can be **linked** to external data from a variety of other applications. Linking an object means that the data is not actually stored with the slide and the source data can be opened directly from *PowerPoint*. If the source data changes, the changes can be reflected automatically on the slide. If the source data is deleted, the text will no longer be available in the slide.

Manoeuvres

1. At the end of the **Links** presentation, create a new **Title Only** slide and add the title **Linked Text**.
2. To create the link, select **Insert | Object** and the **Create from file** option.
3. Click **Browse** and locate the data files. Select the **Labradors** file.
4. Click **OK** and in the **Insert Object** dialog box, check **Link**.

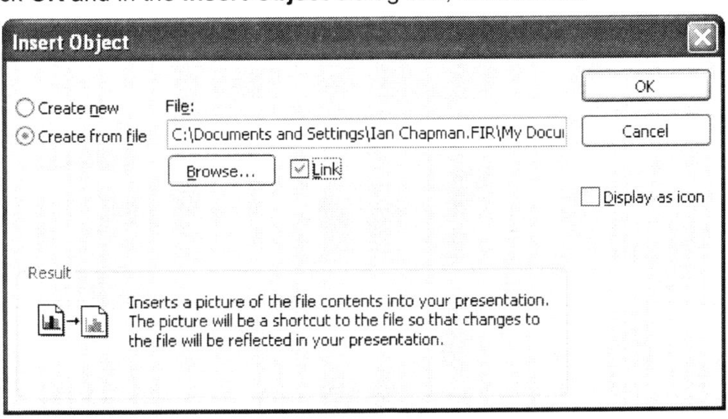

*If **Display as icon** is checked, the text will be displayed on the slide as an icon. In **Normal View**, double clicking the icon will open the source object. In a slide show, this text cannot be accessed.*

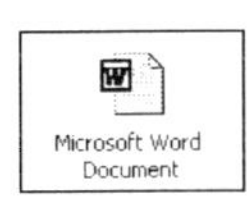

5. Click **OK** to insert the linked object and then save the presentation.
6. To edit the document, double click the text on the slide. *Word* starts and opens the original source document.
7. Select the heading **Our Sanctuary** and make it italic. Save the **Labradors** document and close *Word*. Notice the change is also shown on the slide.
8. Leave the presentation open.

Driving Lesson 51 - Linking to a Chart

Park and Read

Data can be imported into *PowerPoint* from spreadsheets. Rather than create a chart from scratch, if a suitable one already exists within a workbook you can create a link to it.

Manoeuvres

1. At the end of the **Links** presentation, create a new **Title Only** slide and add the title **Linked Chart**.
2. Start *Excel* and open the workbook **Numbers** from the data files.
3. With the **Admittances** sheet tab selected, click **Copy**, 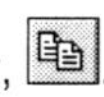.
4. Use the **Taskbar** to return to *PowerPoint*.
5. With the **Linked Chart** slide selected, select **Edit | Paste Special** and select **Paste link**. Do not check **Display as icon**.

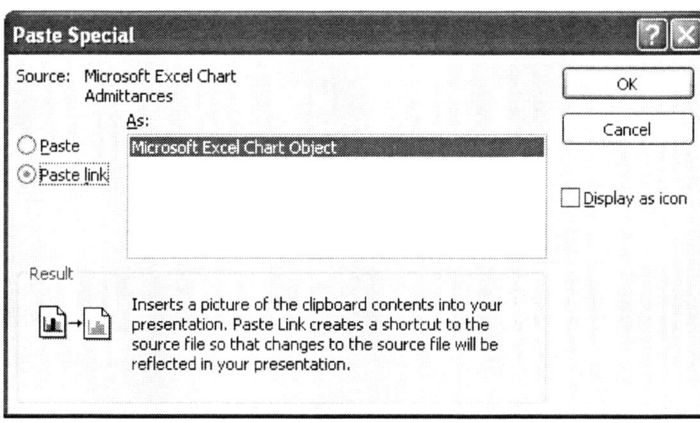

6. Click **OK** to paste the linked chart on to the slide.
7. Save the presentation and leave it open.
8. Leave the *Excel* spreadsheet open.

Driving Lesson 52 - Linking to a Worksheet Range

Park and Read

A link can be created from a slide to a specific range of data on a worksheet.

Manoeuvres

1. At the end of the **Links** presentation create a new **Title Only** slide and add the title **Linked Range**.
2. Use the **Taskbar** to return to the **Numbers** workbook.
3. Press <**Esc**> to remove the marquee (dotted line) on the **Admittances** tab and select the **Data** tab.
4. Click and drag to select the range **B3:D15**.
5. Copy the range and switch back to *PowerPoint*.
6. To link to the range, select **Edit | Paste Special**. Select the **Paste link** option and click **OK**.

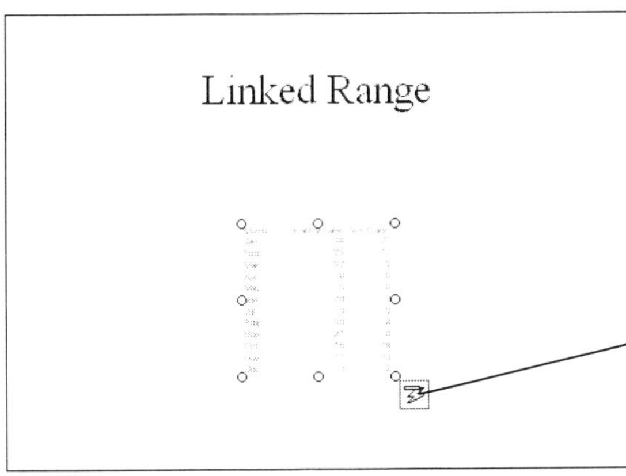

*This **Smart Tag** may or may not be visible, depending on settings chosen*

*To embed a range, select **Edit | Paste**. The figures will not then be updated if the source worksheet is changed.*

7. The range selected from the spreadsheet is now linked to the presentation. This will be demonstrated in a later Driving Lesson.
8. Enlarge the range object by dragging a corner handle then save the presentation.
9. Leave *Excel* and the presentation open.

Driving Lesson 53 - Linking to an Image File

Park and Read

Images can also be linked in a presentation. They can be linked using **Insert | Picture** or **Insert | Object**. If the original image is edited in any way, the changes are reflected in the linked *PowerPoint* object.

Manoeuvres

1. At the end of the **Links** presentation create another **Title Only** slide and name it **Linked Image**.
2. To create the link, select **Insert | Object** and the **Create from file** option.
3. Click **Browse** and locate the supplied data files. Select the **catlink** file.
4. Click **OK** and in the **Insert Object** dialog box, check **Link**.
5. Click **OK** to insert the linked object.

*It may be necessary to use different method to create links to other types of image file, i.e. Select **Insert | Picture**, select the image file, click the drop down arrow on the **Insert** button and select **Link to File**. An image linked in this way will not appear in the **Links** dialog box, see Driving Lesson 55, so the link cannot be controlled.*

6. The linked image is placed on the slide and can be manipulated like any inserted object. Enlarge the image slightly and position it in the centre of the slide.
7. Save the presentation.
8. Close the presentation, but leave *Excel* open.

Driving Lesson 54 - Modifying Linked Data

Park and Read

Whenever a presentation containing links is opened, you will always be prompted to update the links. If the option is accepted, all linked objects within the presentation will be updated with the current versions from the source data. If not, they will be left unchanged.

Manoeuvres

1. If the *Excel* spreadsheet **Numbers** is not open, then open it.
2. Select the worksheet **Admittances**.
3. Double click on any data series for **Healthy Cats** (the lighter colour).
4. To change the colour of the data series, with the **Patterns** tab of the **Format Data Series** dialog box selected, choose yellow from the **Area** colour grid.

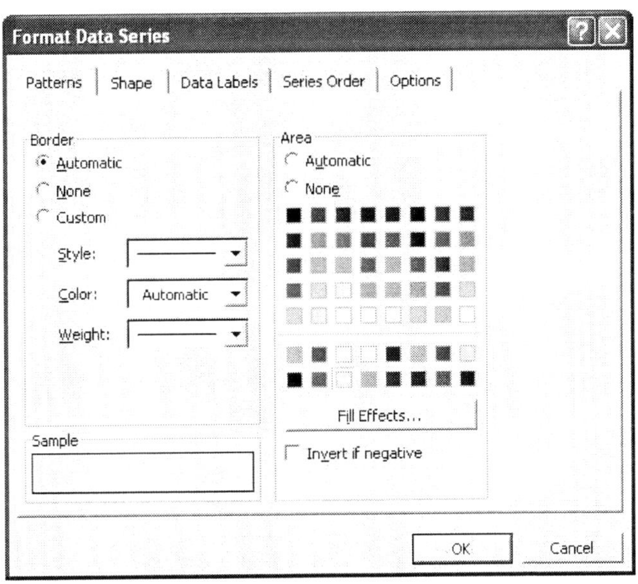

5. Click **OK**.
6. Select the worksheet **Data** and change the **March** figure for **Healthy Cats** to **20**.
7. Save the spreadsheet and close *Excel*.

Driving Lesson 54 - Continued

8. Open *Word* and open the document **Labradors**. Add the text '**This shelter is now closed**.' after the first paragraph.

9. Save the document with the same name and close *Word*.

10. Open *Microsoft Paint*, (**All Programs | Accessories | Paint** from the **Start** menu) and open the image **catlink** from the supplied data files. Remember to specify **All Files** in the **Files of type** box.

11. Use the **Fill with Color** tool to change its colour from black to yellow.

12. Save the image and close the application.

13. In *PowerPoint* open the presentation **Links** - the following prompt appears:

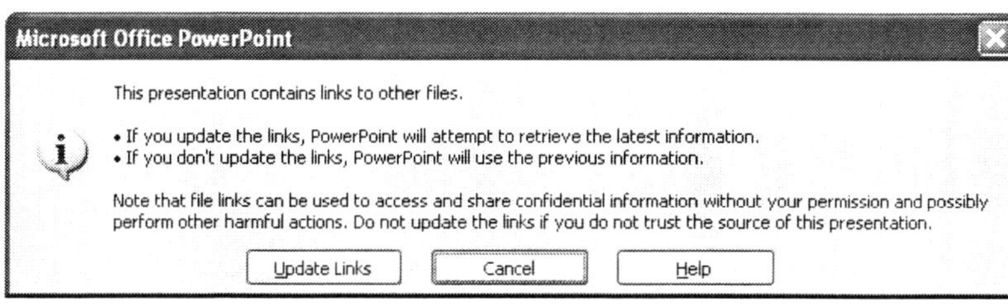

14. Click **Update Links**.

15. View slide **9 Embedded Text** to see that the text is unchanged.

16. View slide **10 Linked Text** to see that the text added in *Word* has also been changed in *PowerPoint*.

17. View slide **11 Linked Chart** to see that the data series changed to yellow in *Excel* has also been changed in *PowerPoint*.

18. View slide **12 Linked Range** to see the amended March figure for **Healthy Cats** in the table.

19. View slide **13 Linked Image** to see that the change in image colour is also shown in *PowerPoint*.

20. Save the presentation.

21. Leave it open for the next Driving Lesson.

Driving Lesson 55 - Managing Links

Park and Read

When an object is **embedded** in a slide, it will <u>not</u> change if the source file is amended. The default for inserting or pasting objects into a presentation is for them to be embedded. To change a linked object to an embedded object the link must be broken.

Manoeuvres

1. In the **Links** presentation, select **Edit | Links**. All links in the presentation are displayed (images linked using **Insert | Picture**, will not appear).

2. Select the **Document** link and click the **Manual** option at the bottom of the dialog box. The file is still linked, but will only ever be updated when manually triggered from this dialog box.

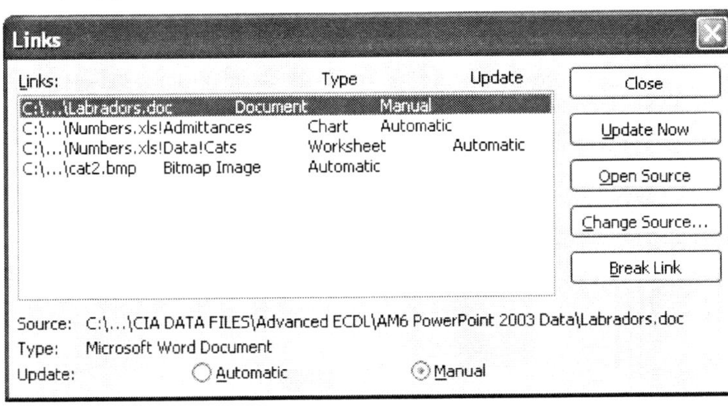

3. To update the document link, make sure it is selected and click **Update Now**. Any current changes in the **Labradors** document will immediately be reflected in the presentation.

4. To break the link to the chart, make sure **Chart** is selected from the list and click **Break Link**. Any changes to the original chart in the **Numbers** spreadsheet will now <u>not</u> be reflected in the presentation.

__Change Source__ is usually used to change the link path when the source document has been moved to a new location.

5. Click **Close** to close the **Links** dialog box. Select slide **11**, **Linked Chart** and double click on the chart. It is now a fixed picture and no longer linked to a spreadsheet. Click **Cancel** to close the **Format Picture** dialog box.

6. Save and close the presentation.

Driving Lesson 56 - Saving a Slide as an Image

Park and Read

As well as using objects in slides, slides themselves can be used as objects within other applications. The easiest way to do this is to save the slide as an image file. This can then be manipulated using image processing programs and inserted into other applications such as *Word* or *Access,* or used in web pages.

Manoeuvres

1. Open the presentation **CIA Seminar** and display slide **3**, the organisation chart, in **Normal View**.
2. Select **File | Save As**.
3. Select the location of the supplied data files in the **Save in** box, enter a **File name** of **Organisation**, and click the drop down arrow in the **Save as type** box.
4. There are options to save the slide as an image file, including **GIF**, **JPEG** or **Bitmap** file formats. Select **GIF Graphics Interchange Format** (may be shown as just **GIF**, or similar).

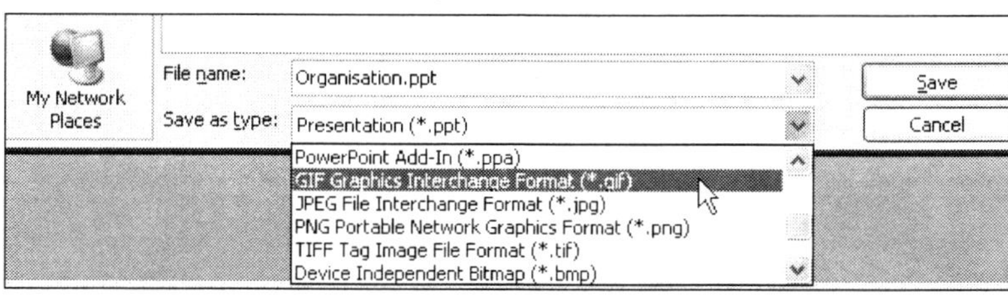

5. Click **Save**. There is a prompt to save all slides in the presentation. Click **Current Slide Only** to save only the selected slide.

*To save all slides, select **Every Slide** and then click **OK**. If all slides are saved, they will be saved as individual images within a folder.*

6. Close the presentation and open *Word.*
7. On a new blank document type the line **Here is our new company structure**.
8. Use **Insert | Picture | From File** to insert the newly created **Organisation.gif** file under the text line.
9. Resize the image to half its size by dragging one of the corner handles and move the image to the centre of the page.
10. Save the document in the data folder as **New Structure** and close *Word.*

Driving Lesson 57 - Revision

This is not an ECDL test. Testing may only be carried out through certified ECDL test centres. This covers the features introduced in this section. Try not to refer to the preceding Driving Lessons while completing it.

1. Open the presentation **Holiday Choice** and save it as **Revision57**.
2. Create a **Title Only** slide at the end of the presentation.
3. Enter the title **More Information Below**.
4. Create a link to the *Word* document **Abseiling** from the data files.
5. Make the linked document as large as possible without obscuring the title.
6. After this slide, insert another **Title Only** slide.
7. Enter the title **You'll be abseiling here**.
8. Insert the **canyon** image, as a linked object on this slide.
9. Resize the graphic until it is double its original size.
10. Move the graphic to the centre of the slide.
11. View the slide show.
12. Save **Slide 2** as a **JPEG** image file, called **Beach.jpg**.
13. Save the changes to the presentation.
14. Close the presentation.

If you experienced any difficulty completing this Revision refer back to the Driving Lessons in this section. Then redo the Revision.

Driving Lesson 58 - Revision

This is not an ECDL test. Testing may only be carried out through certified ECDL test centres. This covers the features introduced in this section. Try not to refer to the preceding Driving Lessons while completing it.

1. Create a new, blank presentation with a **Title Slide**.
2. Enter the title **World Rainfall** and click where indicated to add the subtitle **An Interesting Presentation!**
3. Insert a new **Title Only** slide with the title **London**.
4. Open the *Excel* workbook **Wet**. Copy the **London Rainfall** chart and paste it as a link into the **London** slide. Do not display the chart as an icon.
5. After slide **2** in the presentation, create another **Title Only** slide named **Mumbai**.
6. Paste the **Mumbai Rainfall** chart as a link into the new slide.
7. Save the presentation as **Linked Rainfall** and close it.
8. In *Excel*, select the **Data** sheet in the workbook.
9. Mumbai's monsoon lasted into October. Change the appropriate **Rainfall** figure to **20**.
10. Change the colour of the **Mumbai Rainfall** data series to **Green**.
11. Change the colour of the data series in the **London Rainfall** chart to **Red**.
12. Save the workbook and close *Excel*.
13. Open the presentation **Linked Rainfall**, selecting to update the links when prompted.
14. Check that the charts reflect all the latest changes made to the workbook.
15. Embed the charts by breaking all links.
16. Save the presentation and then close it.

If you experienced any difficulty completing this Revision refer back to the Driving Lessons in this section. Then redo the Revision.

Once you are confident with the features, complete the Record of Achievement Matrix referring to the section at the end of the guide.

Answers

Driving Lesson 11

Step 1 A presentation can be viewed on screen, on an overhead projector, on 35mm slides or as web pages.

Step 2 No, because you must take into account the background, age, occupation and previous knowledge of each audience and tailor the presentation to their needs.

Step 3 Too many colours may distract the audience from the point of the slide.

Step 4 Colour combinations must be chosen carefully as some may be difficult for people with colour blindness to see. Using dark text on a dark background, or light text on a light background, may also cause problems.

Step 5 Colour gradients, patterns, textures and pictures can be used as background effects.

Step 8 No, the new slide is automatically converted to the design of the existing presentation.

Driving Lesson 23

Step 11 Parts of the image could now be recoloured if desired.

Glossary

Action Button	A button placed on a slide that can have actions attached such as navigating to another slide, or presentation, opening another application or playing a sound clip.
Arrange	To position overlapping objects in relation to each other. They can be brought forward or sent backward, or placed on the top or bottom of the pile.
AutoShapes	Ready-made shapes in a variety of categories, which are available from a menu on the **Drawing** toolbar.
Chart Effects	Custom animations that are specific to elements within a chart.
Colour Scheme	A set of pre-defined colours applied to specific areas of a slide.
Combination Chart	A chart which shows different types of information by using two or more chart types. Sometimes called a mixed chart.
Convert	To change the nature of certain graphic images so that they become the same as drawn objects. Done by ungrouping and then grouping a single, selected picture. This cannot be done to bitmap images.
Cropping	A process which allows only a selected part of an image to be displayed.
Custom Animation	Allows the appearance, movement and sound effects attached to any slide object to be specified and customised.
Custom Show	A subset of slides within a show that can be created to be relevant to a specific target audience.
Design Template	A pre-set design, including colours and fonts, that can be applied to slides.
Drawing Objects	Objects that can be created directly on the slide using tools on the **Drawing** Toolbar.
Embedded Object	An object on a slide is described as embedded if it is not linked to a source file.
Flip	To create a mirror-image of an object around its horizontal or vertical axis.
Flowchart	A diagram using pre-set **AutoShapes** to illustrate systems, processes or procedures.
Group	To place two or more selected objects into a group, which is then treated as a single object.
Hyperlink	A link attached to a selected object or piece of text that when clicked in **Slide Show** view, navigates to another location within the same slide, a different slide, a different presentation or application. Hyperlinks can also be attached to e-mail or web site addresses.

Linking	Data from external sources (e.g. text, data, charts etc.) can be linked (different from hyperlinking) to *PowerPoint* slides so that any changes to the source data is automatically applied to the object on the slide.
Mixed Chart	See combination chart.
Position	A setting available within the **Format** dialog box for any object, that allows its precise position to be specified as a pair of measurements from either the top left or centre of the slide.
Presentation	A collection of slides used by a speaker as a visual aid.
Save as an Image	An entire presentation, or the currently selected slide within a presentation, can be saved as a graphic image to be used as an object within other applications.
Slide Layout	The type of slide specified; e.g. **Bulleted List**, **Title Only** etc.
Slide Master	A view that is used to specify settings/formatting and/or objects that will appear on every slide except the **Title Master**.
Slide Show	A presentation being run on screen, with all effects, transitions, sounds, etc.
Template	A presentation framework containing formatting, saved so that it can be used as the basis for future presentations.
Title Master	A view that is used to specify settings/formatting and/or objects that will appear on every slide which is based on the **Title Slide** layout.
Transitions	Special effects that occur as one slide changes to the next during a **Slide Show**. Timings and sound effects may be specified as well as visual effects.
Ungroup	To return a previously grouped set of objects back to acting as individual objects.
Views	Different ways of looking at the slides within a presentation.

Index

Record of Achievement Matrix

This Matrix is to be used to measure your progress while working through the guide. This is a learning reinforcement process, you judge when you are competent.

Tick boxes are provided for each feature. 1 is for no knowledge, 2 some knowledge and 3 is for competent. A section is only complete when column 3 is completed for all parts of the section.

This is not an ECDL test. Testing may only be carried out through certified ECDL test centres.

Tick the Relevant Boxes **1**: No Knowledge **2**: Some Knowledge **3**: Competent

Section	No	Driving Lesson	1	2	3
1 Preparation	1	Design Considerations			
	2	Colour Schemes & Accessibility			
	3	Background Effects			
	4	The Slide Master			
	5	Bullet Levels			
	6	The Title Master			
	7	Creating a Template			
	8	Using a Template			
	9	Inserting Text			
	10	Inserting Slides			
2 Images & Drawn Objects	13	Drawing Objects			
	14	Object Backgrounds			
	15	Rotating or Flipping Objects			
	16	Recolouring Pictures			
	17	Converting Pictures			
	18	Background Graphics			
	19	Arranging Objects			
	20	Cropping Images			
	21	Editing Images			
	22	Different Image Formats			
3 Charts	25	Combination Charts			
	26	Editing Charts			
	27	Animating Charts			
	28	Creating a Flowchart			
	29	Amending a Flowchart			
	30	Creating Other Diagrams			
4 Multimedia	33	Inserting Sounds			
	34	Inserting Movies			
	35	Introducing Animation			
	36	Animation Sequences			

Tick the Relevant Boxes 1: No Knowledge 2: Some Knowledge 3: Competent

Section	No	Driving Lesson	1	2	3
5 Slide Shows	39	Action Buttons			
	40	Editing an Action Button			
	41	Custom Shows			
	42	Running a Custom Show			
	43	Applying Transitions			
	44	Applying Timings			
	45	Setting up a Slide Show			
	46	Slide Show Techniques			
6 Linking	49	Embedding			
	50	Linking Text			
	51	Linking to a Chart			
	52	Linking to a Worksheet Range			
	53	Linking to an Image File			
	54	Modifying Linked Data			
	55	Managing Links			
	56	Saving a Slide as an Image			

Other Products from CiA Training Ltd

CiA Training Ltd is a leading publishing company, which has consistently delivered the highest quality products since 1985. A wide range of flexible and easy to use self teach resources has been developed by CiA's experienced publishing team to aid the learning process. These include the following ECDL Foundation approved products at the time of publication of this product:

- **ECDL/ICDL Syllabus 5.0**
- **ECDL/ICDL Advanced Syllabus 2.0**
- **ECDL/ICDL Revision Series**
- **ECDL/ICDL Advanced Syllabus 2.0 Revision Series**
- **e-Citizen**

Previous syllabus versions also available - contact us for further details.

We hope you have enjoyed using our materials and would love to hear your opinions about them. If you'd like to give us some feedback, please go to:

www.ciatraining.co.uk/feedback.php

and let us know what you think.

New products are constantly being developed. For up to the minute information on our products, to view our full range, to find out more, or to be added to our mailing list, visit:

www.ciatraining.co.uk